HOW TO PREPARE YOUR CURRICULUM VITAE

HOW TO PREPARE YOUR CURRICULUM VITAE

Second Edition

Acy L. Jackson

VGM Career Horizons
NTC/Contemporary Publishing Company

Library of Congress Cataloging-in-Publication Data

Jackson, Acy L.
    How to prepare your curriculum vitae / Acy L. Jackson.—2nd ed.
      p.   cm.
    ISBN 0-8442-4130-X (alk. paper)
    1. Résumés (Employment).   I. Title.
HF5383.J24   1993
  650.14—dc20
                                           96-26637
                                             CIP

Published by VGM Career Horizons
An imprint of NTC/Contemporary Publishing Company
4255 West Touhy Avenue, Lincolnwood (Chicago), Illinois 60646-1975 U.S.A.
Copyright © 1997 by NTC/Contemporary Publishing Company
Printed in the United States of America
International Standard Book Number: 0-8442-4130-X

18 17 16 15 14 13 12 11 10 9 8 7 6 5 4 3 2

Contents

Dedication

To

Charlie Jackson
my father

Ollie Green Jackson
my mother

Tsekani Allette-Jackson
my son

Jamil Allette-Jackson
my grandson

whose love, devotion, and inspiration continue to sustain
me through my most stimulating and creative moments

Acknowledgments

I am deeply indebted to Roberta J. Walmer, of Terra Community College (Fremont, OH), for invaluable assistance in editing and revising the information for this edition. Without her exceptional editing skills and keen understanding of content and format appropriate for a quality CV, this effort would not have been completed. I am also very grateful to Benedict Umezurike for assistance in crafting the sample CV in anthropology and Oindrila Sen for assistance in preparing the sample CV in mathematics.

To Betsy Lancefield, Associate Editor of VGM Career Books, I offer my sincere appreciation for her patience and sage advice in the completion of this revision.

Acy L. Jackson

About the Author

Acy L. Jackson is president of ACY L. JACKSON & Associates, which provides career, interpersonal, and intercultural consultation services for private sector employers and educational institutions. He was associate dean of students and director of the Career Planning Center at Colgate University in Hamilton, New York. In these capacities he counseled students and young professionals who applied to graduate and professional schools, sought employment, and/or applied for graduate fellowships. He was also a part-time instructor at the English Language Institute at Syracuse University.

Prior to Colgate, Mr. Jackson was associate dean of students, director of the career planning and placement center, and instructor-at-large at the College of Wooster in Ohio. He was director of Armaghan English Language Institute in Tehran, Iran, and taught English at a boarding school in West Pakistan.

Jackson holds a B.B.A. degree from Westminster College (PA), an M.Ed. from the University of Pittsburgh, and an M.A. from Teachers College, Columbia University. Selected as a participant in the Institute for Educational Management at Harvard University in 1985, he received the Administrative Development Award from Colgate University that year. He has served as distinguished instructor of career life planning for the American Management Association's Operation Enterprise Program.

Jackson has published articles on teaching English as a foreign language and career planning for undergraduates. In fall 1989, he was one of three Americans selected to participate in an international seminar on career planning and placement at the University of Oxford in England.

Introduction

The curriculum vitae, commonly referred to as a CV, Vita, or Vitae, is a brief biographical résumé of one's educational and work background. The origin of the term is Latin and means "the course of one's life or career."

The curriculum vitae, long in use among professionals in higher education, is gaining currency among undergraduates applying for admission to graduate and professional schools as well as for selected areas of employment. Moreover, because of the growing tendency to use brief applications—often only two pages long—some graduate and professional programs actually encourage applicants to enclose a CV with their applications. For this reason, the curriculum vitae is often referred to as an "academic résumé."

How to Prepare Your Curriculum Vitae provides effective and timely guidelines for about-to-be college graduates, for continuing graduate students, and for professionals who need to update an existing CV or, in planning a career transition, need to prepare one. It is especially suited to the needs of faculty and staff who provide academic, personal, and career/vocational counseling.

1
Getting Started: The Emotional Dimension

The process of writing a curriculum vitae can be an exhilarating experience because it generates a heightened degree of pride in your accomplishments and achievements. You should therefore begin the process with enthusiasm and a desire to share information about yourself. If you approach this process with anxiety or uncertainty about its efficacy, writing a curriculum vitae will not be a pleasurable experience.

If you are like most individuals, you will probably experience a mixture of emotions ranging from nonchalance to denial of the need to prepare a CV. You will probably have emotional highs and lows that will affect every aspect of the work to be accomplished. It is therefore essential to recognize that your feelings about yourself have much to do with the degree of confidence with which you approach and effectively complete this process. In that respect, a minicounseling exercise may well be in order.

View the process of preparing an effective CV as more than merely recording your educational and work background. Instead, make it an intensely satisfying experience by critically reflecting upon your life. In this frame of mind then, consider the following suggestions as an intellectual and emotional foundation for the preparation of your CV. Find a quiet place and allow yourself sufficient time to ponder and identify your reactions, and then record them on the following pages. Return to this chapter whenever a source of personal support is needed. Revisions, additions, and clarifications will occur naturally as your work progresses.

1. Why are you writing a curriculum vitae?

    _____

    _____

    _____

    _____

    _____

    _____

    _____

    _____

    _____

    _____

2. Describe your feelings as you begin this process.

    _____

    _____

    _____

    _____

    _____

    _____

    _____

    _____

    _____

    _____

3. The preparation for writing a curriculum vitae can engender feelings of self-analysis and self-evaluation. Describe your responses to these forms of reflection.

    _____

    _____

    _____

    _____

    _____

    _____

    _____

    _____

    _____

    _____

4. It is essential that you confront any uneasiness, discomfort, or negative feelings you have about your background. Write them down and then set them aside. Do not dwell on them.

_____

_____

_____

_____

_____

_____

_____

_____

_____

_____

5. List your strengths and document each with an experience in which you take great pride.

_____

_____

_____

_____

_____

_____

_____

_____

_____

_____

≣ 2 ≣
The Electronic
Curriculum Vitae

In keeping with the bold innovations in telecommunications, a revolution of monumental proportions is occurring in the job search process. While recent developments are having a profound impact on the way major corporations first screen applicants for positions, the ripple effects are being felt not only by prospective employers in small- to medium-size organizations but also in the ways in which individuals prepare information to present themselves as applicants for positions. The revolution involves computers, which are now setting the standard by which information is processed and presented to decision makers.

As you prepare your curriculum vitae and its accompanying correspondence, it is essential that you prepare two copies of your material; one for people to read and one to be scanned by a computer. Not surprisingly, the computer that drives the new technology defines the terms and sets the structure and guidelines for the information it will accept or reject. For example, traditionally, hiring professionals expected applicants to use action verbs to describe what they had done or could do. In the new mode, individuals are required to use nouns or job titles, as computers are programmed to scan CVs for certain proscribed ideal characteristics in applicants. These nouns or ideal characteristics are called *keywords*. In scannable résumés and CVs, these words appear in prescribed positions at the beginning of the document.

At the forefront of this new technology is the program by Resumix Corporation of Santa Clara, California, which offers a free copy of its brochure, "Preparing the Ideal Scannable Resume." For a copy, send a legal size, self-addressed, stamped envelope to: Resumix, Pamphlet Offer, 2953 Bunker Hill Lane, Santa Clara, CA 95054.

There are two other publications that have anticipated and essentially defined this emerging electronic revolution. They are:

- Kennedy, Joyce Lain and Thomas J. Morrow.
  The Electronic Resume Revolution. second edition. New York: John Wiley & Sons, 1995.

- Kennedy, Joyce Lain and Thomas J. Morrow.
  The Electronic Job Search Revolution. New York: John Wiley & Sons, 1994.

FEATURES OF THE IDEAL SCANNABLE CURRICULUM VITAE[1]

1. Scannable CVs focus on clearly defined format and content rules which are determined by Optical Character Recognition. OCR creates a text file in ASCII (American Standard Code for Information Interchange). Next, artificial intelligence reads the text and extracts the information it needs.

2. A CV to be scannable has to be clean and crisp with dark type—preferably standard fonts—so that OCR can recognize every letter.

TIPS FOR WRITING A SCANNABLE CURRICULUM VITAE

- Use the language and acronyms appropriate for the field in which you are seeking entry.

- Use commonly accepted headings for the sections.

- Use active verbs when noting responsibilities and skills.

- Include keywords when describing your skills, education, and experience; be specific.

- Be honest and succinct.

- Your CV may exceed one page, as the computer's ability to scan it is not affected by length.

---

1. Adapted from "Preparing the Ideal Scannable Resume." Resumix Corporation, 1995.

Tips for Producing a Scannable Curriculum Vitae

- The original should be letter quality.

- Use a standard typeface in a font size of 10 to 14 points.

- Use standard spacing; letters should not touch.

- Avoid using italics, underlining, lines, graphics, two-column format, or boxes. Emphasize using bold or full capitalization.

- Your name should be at the top of the first page, followed by your address beneath it. Each phone number should be on a separate line. Successive pages should have your name as the first text.

- Do not fold or staple.

Sample Scannable Curricula Vitae

The format and design of the following scannable CVs adhere to guidelines established by Joyce Lain Kennedy and Thomas J. Morrow in their pioneering publication, *Electronic Resume Revolution* second edition. New York: John Wiley & Sons, Inc., 1995.

MOIRA ELSPETH SOAMES

Big Sky Ranch • Jackson Hole, WY 82072 • 307 765-6029
maisonette theasthai • Savannah, GA 31401 • 912 262-0015
Messages: 912 267-0000
E-Mail: http://www.soames

KEYWORD PROFILE　　Actress. Toy Designer. Producer. Writer. Cartoonist. Film Maker. Dancer. Fundraiser. Suburban Teens. Substance Abuse. Fitness. Dependability. Mature Judgment. High Energy. Creative. Flexible. Sensitive. Competitive. Detail Minded. Public Speaking. Organizational Skills. Results Oriented. Team Player. Ensemble. MFA Degree. BFA Degree. University of Wisconsin-Madison. Video Production. West Virginia University. Professional Diploma in Film Production. Presidential Scholar in the Arts. University Scholar. National Endowment for the Arts Administrative Fellows Program.

OBJECTIVE　　A fund raising position for ensemble productions of documentaries depicting quality fitness and nutrition programs for suburban teens engaged in substance abuse.

EXPERIENCE

1994-Present **Production Intern/Assistant Development Officer**. The American Place Theatre. New York, NY. Assisted production manager in rehearsals and running of productions; solicited corporate foundations for financial support of theatre productions; raised $95,000 for annual theatre summer festival productions.

1992-1994 **Associate Stage Manager/Public Relations Specialist**. Circle Repertory Company, New York, NY. Managed development projects; supervised backstage crew of eighteen; assisted stage manager in twelve productions; made monthly appearances on public television to solicit funds for theatre productions.

1991-1992 **Assistant Literary/Dramaturg**. The Guthrie Theatre, Minneapolis, MN. Researched current productions; wrote articles for theatre productions.

Summer 1991 **Production Assistant**. Castillo Video, Albuquerque, NM. Assisted in production of cable television shows, documentaries, and special events; duties included camera work, editing, research, and administrative support.

Summer 1992 **Associate Computer Games Specialist**. Lucasdigital Ltd., Lucusfilm Ltd., Lucasarts Entertainment Co., San Raphael, CA. Assisted game developers and game artists in developing computer software games; utilized 2-D computer graphic art/animation techniques in producing computer games.

EDUCATION

1992, **Professional Diploma in Film Production**, Honors, University of Wisconsin-Madison, Madison, WI.
    Coursework:
- Film Styles and Genres
- Critical Film Analysis
- The American Film Industry in the Age of Television
- Video Production and Direction
- Advanced Motion Picture Production
- Film Colloquium
- Seminar - Radio Television Film
- Seminar in Film Theory

    Recipient, The E. B. Fred Fellowship

1990, **Master of Fine Arts**, High Honors, West Virginia University, Morgantown, WV.
Major: Acting
    Coursework:
- Directed Theatre Studies
- Advanced Technical Theatre
- Costume History
- Creative Dramatics
- Puppetry
- Advanced Playwriting
- Classic Theatre
- Advanced Graduate Vocal Techniques
- Graduate Stage Movement
- Advanced Graduate Stage Movement
- Graduate Acting Studio
- Period Style
- Graduate Colloquium

    Recipient, W. E. B. DuBois Fellowship; Arlen G. and Louise Stone Swiger Fellowship.

MOIRA ELSPETH SOAMES
page three

1987, **Bachelor of Fine Arts**, cum laude, Fashion Institute of Fine Arts, New York, NY. Major: toy design Minor: dance.

SCHOLARSHIPS

1991, **Presidential Scholar in the Arts Award**, Presidential Scholar in the Arts Recognition and Talent Search. Awarded by the National Foundation for Advancement in the Arts (NFAA). Honoured at the White House and received $1000.

1993, **National Ten-Minute Play Contest**, Actors Theatre of Louisville, Louisville, KY. One-act play "Love au gratin."

AFFILIATIONS

American Film Institute
Association of Visual Communicators
Toy Manufacturers of America
USITT: The American Association of Design and Production Professionals in the Performing Arts

MENZIES H. QING

3401 Assylum Avenue
Hartford, CT 06705

203 768-1900
E-mail: Menzies@mail.hartford.per

Keywords

Television. Theology. Religion. Philosophy. Culture. Chinese. PhD Harvard University. MDiv Graduate Theological Union. BA University of Melbourne. Australia. WPIX-TV Channel 11. WIHN-TV. WTNH-TV Channel 8. CBS "60 Minutes." Talk Show Host. Copy Editor. Researcher. Interviewer. Charlie Rose. Oprah Winfrey. Mike Wallace. WordPerfect 6.0. WordPerfect for Windows. Communication Skills. Accurate. Adaptable. Aggressive Work. Analytical Ability. Conceptual Ability. Articulate. Creative. Public Speaking. High Energy. Persuasive. Tenacious.

Professional Objective

A position as host of a television program which presents discourse on philosophical, theological, and religious perspectives of cultures in America.

Education

1995 PhD, **HARVARD UNIVERSITY**, Cambridge, MA
Major: Systematic and Philosophical Theology and Philosophy of Religion
Dissertation: "Theological and Philosophical Perspectives of God and Man in the Writings of Paul Tillich and Pierre Teilhard de Chardin"
Coursework:
- Themes in African American Religious History
- Current Trends in American Judaism
- Aramaic/Rabbinic Hebrew
- Hermeneutics and Christian Theories: A Historical Survey
- Theories of Religion and Culture
- Medieval Religious Texts
- World Religions
- Otherness and History in the Study of Religion
- Seminar in Systematic Philosophy
- Advanced Problems in Philosophy of Language
- Observation and Interpretation of Religious Action
- Seminar in Philosophical Theology
- Islam

MENZIES H. QING   2

1990 MDiv, **GRADUATE THEOLOGICAL UNION**, Berkeley, CA
      Major: Cultural and Historical Study of Religion
      Thesis: "History of Religion in America: 1970-1980"
      Coursework:
- Religion, Fundamentalism and Nationalism
- Modern Western Religious Thought
- Religion and Anthropology
- History of Religion in America Since 1865
- Ethnicity, Race, and Religion in America
- Public Religion in US History
- Sufism
- Topics in Comparative Religions
- Buddhism
- Understanding World Religions in Multicultural Contexts

1987 BA, **UNIVERSITY OF MELBOURNE**, Melbourne, Australia
      Major: Asian Languages and Literatures
      Specialty: Chinese Language and Literatures

Awards

January 1995 **Beinecke Library Short-Term Fellowship**, Yale University.
      Researched publications in medieval philosophy in the Beinecke Rare Book
      and Manuscript Library.

1984 **Sidney E. Mead Prize**. Awarded for best essay - "History of Religion in
      America: 1960-1970" - in the field of church history by a doctoral
      candidate.

Experience

1995 **Researcher**, "The Charlie Rose Show," WCNY-TV, New York, NY. Reviewed
      publications and prepared notes for program.

Summer 1994 **Copy Editor**, "60 Minutes," CBS TELEVISION. Prepared information
      for Mike Wallace's segments of programs.

1994 **Interviewer/Prompter**, "The Oprah Winfrey Show," ABC TELEVISION.
      Interviewed guests who appeared on the show.

Summer 1993 **Newscaster**, WTNH-TV Channel 8, Hartford, CT. Weekend news
      co-anchor.

Summer 1992 **Newscaster**, WPIX-TV Channel 11, New York, NY. Weekend news
      co-anchor.

MENZIES H. QING   3

1989-1991 **Intern/Panelist**, AUSTRALIAN BROADCASTING COMPANY, New York, NY. Panelist on programs describing American culture for broadcast in Australia; edited scripts for guests.

Summer 1988 **Model**, THE de l'Orme AGENCY, Boston, MA. Appeared on television in automobile commercials.

Skills

Language: Conversationally fluent in Chinese
                 Proficient in French

Computer: Software and programming in C, C++, and visual BASIC in Windows NT and WNIX environments

Interests

Chinese language and theatre; Dead Sea Scrolls; theology; sailing; swimming; television

CHECKLIST FOR PREPARATION OF SCANNABLE CURRICULA VITAE[2]

1. _____ Select keywords carefully and arrange them in an order that complements the categories of your CV. They should not only appear in the KEYWORD category but also in other parts of your CV. (Consult *The Electronic Resume Revolution* for guidance in using keywords.)

2. _____ Use a popular, common typeface such as Helvetica, Futura, Optima, Univers, Times, Palatino, or Courier.

3. _____ Use a font size between 10 points and 14 points. Your name, however, should always appear in a font at the upper end of this range.

4. _____ Avoid italics, script, and underlined passages.

5. _____ Do not use graphics and shading.

6. _____ Use horizontal and vertical lines sparingly. If you use them, however, allow a quarter-inch of white space around them.

7. _____ Use a 24-pin letter quality or laser printer.

8. _____ Use 8 1/2 × 11 inch white paper.

9. _____ Place your name at the very top of your CV. It must be on a line by itself.

10. _____ Avoid stapling or folding your CV.

Additional checklist items from Resumix Educational Services, Resumix, Inc., 1994.[3]

11. _____ Use boldface and/or all capital letters as long as the letters do not touch each other.

---

2. Adapted from Kennedy and Morrow. *The Electronic Resume Revolution*. second edition. New York: John Wiley & Sons, 1995.

3. "Preparing the Ideal Scannable Resume," available free from Resumix Pamphlet Offer, 2953 Bunker Hill Lane, Santa Clara, CA 95054. Send a legal size, self-addressed, stamped envelope.

12. _____ Avoid two-column formats.

13. _____ Place your name at the top of the page on its own line. It can also be the first text on pages two and three.

14. _____ Use standard address format below your name.

15. _____ List each phone number on its own line.

16. _____ Do not condense spacing between letters.

≡ 3 ≡
Listing Competencies and Skills

The next stage in the process of preparing a curriculum vitae involves delineating your competencies and skills. Competencies are what a person can do well, and include all the things he or she has learned, as well as skills developed through education, training, and experience. As individuals develop, they acquire credentials, which state what they are able to do and the level of proficiency at which they do it. Credentials usually take the form of diplomas, degrees, licenses, and certificates.[1]

It is not always easy to separate the competencies and skills that are the outcomes of life experiences from those that result from structured educational experiences; most people would insist that life itself is a learning experience. This chapter nonetheless encourages individuals whose experiences allow for such distinctions to do so (see Step III). It provides step-by-step procedures for identifying educational and noneducational competencies and skills that might be listed on your CV.

STEP I: COMPETENCIES

The following classifications are presented as a means of encouraging you to inventory your competencies and present them as effectively as possible on your CV. No effort has been made to define each competency—that would be

---

1. Appalachia Educational Laboratory, Inc. Career Decision-Making Program. *Career Planning and Decision-Making for College*. Bloomington, Illinois: McKnight Publishing Company, 1980.

too restrictive—or place values on any competency or group of competencies. You are expected instead to make broad assessments. Using the list below as a guide, write several statements that describe your competencies. This list deals with perspective—that is, how one sees a situation or how one views what one knows.

— Intellectual disposition	— Maturity
• Imagination	— Cultural perspective
• Curiosity	— Problem-solving
• Commitment	— Discrimination
• Sympathy	— Appetite for discovery
• Excitement (enthusiasm)	— Critical judgment
• Creativity	

The following samples will help guide the development of your self-statements.

Exercise for Step I

Sample #1   sympathy for economically disadvantaged; imaginative in creating scenarios for social change; committed to community involvement in decision-making processes

Sample #2   committed to consensus in policy decisions; utilize effectively mathematical and quantitative reasoning in marketing strategies; enthusiastic about profits; employ state-of-the-art communication techniques to interpersonal interactions

#1

#2

#3

#4

#5

STEP II: CREDENTIALS

In this step you need to provide information regarding your degrees, licenses, and certificates. You should also consider the experiences that were an integral part of your acquisition of these credentials and list some of the outcomes of your participation in these programs. In short, ask yourself what skills you have developed from the credentials you have acquired.

Exercise for Step II

PROFESSIONAL degree (for example, architecture, business, law, medicine)

Outcomes:

POSTGRADUATE (certificate)

Specialization:

Outcomes:

GRADUATE degree (doctorate)

Specialization:

Outcomes:

GRADUATE degree (master)

Majors:

Minors:

Outcomes:

UNDERGRADUATE degree (bachelor's)

Majors:

Minors:

Outcomes:

STEP III: SKILLS

Document your skills in the following exercise. Do not be concerned yet about the way they might appear on your CV; the objective here is to generate as much information as possible. An exercise at the end of this chapter will guide you through appropriate revisions of this information for the final draft of your CV. Use the following lists as preliminary guidelines for delineating your skills.

PARA INTELLECTUAL (content, knowledge)
What you know

- A specific body of knowledge
  - Boundaries that divide traditional disciplines

- Mathematical and quantitative reasoning
  - Developing mathematical models
  - Budgeting

- Research
  - Investigation
  - Reading

- Negotiation strategies

- Counseling theories
  - Advising

- Decision making

- Evaluation

- Management

PROCESS (technique or craft)

What you do with what you know, or how you do what you know how to do:

- Written/spoken language
  - Precision
  - Fluency
  - Clarity
  - Persuasion
  - Concision

- Information processing; the ability to
  - Select
  - Interpret
  - Store
  - Place information into a larger context

- Observation

- Logical reasoning

- Historical method

- Scientific method

- Research

- Stimulated listening

- Rhetorical style

- Organization

- Evaluation

- Improvisation

- Analysis/conceptualization

Exercise for Step III

SKILLS	Documentation Context in which skill was developed and in which it is currently being used	
	Education/Training	**Life/Work Experience**
Sample: Language competency	• Advanced Gaelic classes, Dublin University, Dublin, Eire, Ireland • *Tutor*, Beginning Gaelic, Boston College, Chestnut Hill, MA	• *Member*, The Gaelic League, New York, NY • *Assistant Coach*, County Galway, Irish GAILLIMH, Football Team, Galway, Ireland

Step IV: Levels or Degrees of Proficiency

Using the skills you identified in Step III, describe the levels or degrees of proficiency you have achieved in using them. The following list will assist you in completing this exercise. Add other qualifiers that best describe your degree of proficiency in using your skills.

accurate (in)
adept (in, at)
advanced (knowledge of)
alert (in)

_____

_____

_____

concise
competent
conversant (in)

_____

_____

_____

detailed (knowledge of)

_____

_____

_____

effective (in)
empathy
exceptional
exemplary
expert (in, at)
extraordinary

_____

_____

_____

fluent (in)
functions (well)

_____

_____

gifted
good (at)
great

_____

_____

_____

high (degree of)

_____

_____

intermediate (knowledge of)

_____

_____

_____

judicious

_____

_____

_____

keen (sense of, understanding of,
perception of)

_____

_____

_____

_____

master (mastery of)

_____

_____

_____

_____

perceptive
practical (experience in)
proficient (in)

_____

_____

_____

_____

relentless (in pursuit of)
rudimentary

_____

_____

sensitive (to)
skilled (at, in)
sophisticated (understanding of)
strong (sense of, background in,
knowledge of)
successful (in, at)

_____

_____

_____

uncommon
understanding (of)
unusual

_____

_____

_____

Exercise for Step IV

Skill	Level or Degree of Proficiency
Sample: Improvisation (music composition)	Gifted trombonist; Expert in creating extemporaneous jazz idioms using folk elements indigenous to southeastern United States; Master in use of counterpoint rhythms

Step V: Review

Review the worksheets and exercises you have completed in Steps I through IV. Summarize this information by writing your five most important competencies and skills along with the level or degree of proficiency you have achieved in using them. Write them in draft form for now. You will revise them as you complete the information requested in chapter 4.

The following factors might affect the skills and competencies you choose:

- Your career, professional, and/or research objective

- The program or position for which you are preparing your CV

- The degree of importance you attribute to your competencies and skills as a part of the total presentation of yourself

Exercise for Step V

Sample: relentless in pursuit of excellence in instruction; function well in environments that expect high degree of critical judgment, maturity, sympathy, and creativity in instructional methods; keen understanding and appreciation of diverse learning styles; proficient in evaluation of student performance on oral examinations

#1

#2

#3

#4

#5

4

Preparing Working Drafts

Major Components of Curricula Vitae

A curriculum vitae reflects, in the broadest sense, the essence, structure, and components of one's experiences as a graduate with credentials from institutions of higher education. It also includes experiences pursued after such study. There are some common experiences that students and professionals in a wide range of occupations share. These therefore are used as defining characteristics or categories of a curriculum vitae.

Professional/Career/Vocational/Research Objective(s)

Education

Coursework

Honors/Achievements/Awards/Kudos

Thesis/Dissertation Abstract

Research Interest(s)

Research and/or Laboratory Experience

Teaching Interests and Experience

Instrumentation Experience

Special Skills

Publications/Presentations/Works-in-Progress

Work Experience

Professional Associations/Learned and/or Scientific Societies

Background

Community Service

Cocurricular Activities

Interests

Travel

References/Recommendations

These categories are not finite and should be tailored to meet your needs. Adapt them to fit your experiences—use them, in fact, as a basis for creating categories that more precisely fit your own situation.

The order in which these broad categories might appear on your CV should reflect the degree of importance you attribute to them. Arrange them so that the most important information appears at the beginning of your CV and the least important at the end.

In the pages that follow, you will find descriptions of each category and suggestions for preparing **preliminary**, **revised**, and **final versions** of your descriptive information. Use these guidelines as you prepare the initial draft of your curriculum vitae.

1. Do not feel compelled to complete all of the worksheets at one sitting. Begin with those that request routine information and then move on to those that require reflection and detailed organization.

2. Focus on content initially. Describe experiences in detail and later refine them through careful revision.

3. Ignore any overlap between categories. Some duplications or redundancies will be resolved as you work through the drafts. Others can be edited or corrected in consultation with your academic adviser or mentor.

4. There are at least two alternative or complementary electronic approaches to organizing the information in the categories that you might consider.

   • Self-teaching résumé (and curriculum vitae)
   Templates for use with standard word processing programs.

   Yana Parker has developed a comprehensive approach to the preparation of templates, which she describes as detailed structural outlines of documents that provide a starting point and some graphic assistance in visualizing a finished product. These self-teaching templates also provide explicit instructions about the nature of the material to be entered in a particular section or location, along with instructions that link the various parts together to form a focused, coherent, and concise document.[1] She warns that your résumé will not look exactly like the templates and therefore must be customized in the curriculum vitae format. In fact, she offers alternative wording for some categories, as well as optional categories that are clearly appropriate for CVs.

- Use a word processing program to delineate the categories, which will allow for ease in making revisions later.

---

1. Parker, Yana. *Resume Pro: The Professional's Guide*. Berkeley, CA: Ten Speed Press, 1993. Parker's "Self-Teaching Templates for your PC" (for IBM compatibles, in WordPerfect and Microsoft Word (including Windows); for Apple Macintosh, in Microsoft Word) can be ordered from: Yana Parker, (Software Department #10), P.O. Box 3289, Berkeley, CA 94703.

Professional/Career/ Vocational/Research Objective(s)

This category can be as brief as one sentence stating a general goal or as long as a brief paragraph expressing both short-term and/or long-term goals.

Be sure to research carefully all graduate and professional programs and areas of employment that interest you. Make sure that your goals, which should be logical and clearly stated, match those of the program or position for which you are applying.

Finally, avoid vague or obscure language that fails to express precisely what you would like to do.

Preliminary Version

Edited for Revised Version

Edited for Final Version

Education

In this category and the category describing coursework, your objective is to provide graduate and professional schools and prospective employers with a brief but thorough understanding of your academic background. Indicate your graduation dates; the degrees, diplomas, or certificates you have earned; and the names of the universities, colleges, professional schools, or other institutions where you have studied. Include your major and minor along with your grade point averages in each. Also list your cumulative grade point average for each institution attended as well as for each degree.

If you have completed a graduate degree, or coursework toward a graduate or professional degree, that information should precede information on your undergraduate degree(s).

Highlight significant academic achievements, such as strong grade point averages in specific courses, as well as any extensive background you might have in areas of study outside your major and/or minor. If you are an undergraduate and a candidate for honors or high honors in your major, indicate that in this category.

Preliminary Version

Edited for Revised Version

Edited for Final Version

Coursework

Using your most recent transcript(s), list all courses in groups that support and strengthen your professional, career, vocational, and/or research objective(s). Provide complete course titles, with brief descriptions where appropriate. You might also find it worthwhile to list the grades you have received in some courses if you want to highlight academic performance or describe a trend in that performance. Do not include course numbers or abbreviations.

Preliminary Version

Edited for Revised Version

Edited for Final Version

Honors/Achievements/ Awards/Kudos

List and briefly describe all special recognitions, including study group participation; departmental, athletic, and dean's awards; scholarships and fellowships; and community and professional awards. As a general rule, however, do not list high school awards or achievements since they might diminish the importance of undergraduate and graduate awards. If you have significant secondary school awards or achievements you want to include, discuss your ideas with your academic adviser.

Preliminary Version

Edited for Revised Version

Edited for Final Version

Thesis/Dissertation Abstract

This summary statement should be a brief description of your thesis or dissertation, including the full title and date (term) of completion. Consult with your academic adviser regarding the appropriate wording of this statement. Some disciplines (for example, chemistry and psychology) have specific editorial formats for abstracts. Check the thesis or dissertation format for your topic to assure that you use the correct form for the field.

Preliminary Version

Edited for Revised Version

Edited for Final Version

Research Interest(s)

Be as *specific* and *precise* as possible regarding the description of your research interest(s). Strike a balance between being specific enough to ensure congruence between your objectives and those of the program and employment option for which you are submitting your CV and being general enough not to preclude options that you might pursue if you were flexible. The delicate balancing act that is required makes this category extremely complex and thus often requires consultation not only with your academic adviser but also with representatives of graduate and professional schools or with prospective employers.

Preliminary Version

Edited for Revised Version

Edited for Final Version

Research and/or Laboratory Experience

In this category, you need to provide detailed descriptions of your research and laboratory experience. Include information about the ways in which your research or laboratory experience fits into a given profession or into a particular laboratory's ongoing research. Be sure to give the title of each project and information concerning its actual or potential publication. Also, list the names and titles of professors or other individuals who have supervised or are currently supervising your research or laboratory experiences.

Preliminary Version

Edited for Revised Version

Edited for Final Version

Teaching Interests and Experience

For this section, describe only those teaching interests that can be documented by experience. You might also include in this category tutoring experience, as well as any group learning experience in which you were a leader.

Preliminary Version

Edited for Revised Version

Edited for Final Version

Instrumentation Experience

If you have used instruments in a laboratory situation—for example, computer hardware, photographic, or audiovisual equipment—describe that use. You will probably not need to provide extensive detail regarding the instruments themselves. On the other hand, if you have used state-of-the-art instruments, it is appropriate to describe both the instruments and the extent of your use of them.

Preliminary Version

Edited for Revised Version

Edited for Final Version

Special Skills

Use the information you developed in chapter 3 in deciding what to include in this category. Describe in detail any interpersonal, leadership, organizational, or analytical skills you have, and the contexts in which you have used them. Do the same for any languages, computers, computer software, and so on.

Students who intend to pursue graduate study should clearly describe their levels of competency in that particular field. Vague descriptions might be interpreted as a marginal degree of competency. See a list of selected fields of graduate study in appendix F.

Preliminary Version

Edited for Revised Version

Edited for Final Version

Publications/ Presentations/ Works-in-Progress

If you have publications of your own or have coauthored publications with faculty or other colleagues, provide appropriate bibliographic descriptions of them. You should list unpublished manuscripts *only* if they are actually being considered for publication.

Artists and musicians should provide complete descriptions of works-in-progress.

Provide detailed descriptions of presentations, particularly those before academic societies and professional associations. Documentation should include the title of the presentation, the name of the organization, the location of the meeting, and the date. Although classroom presentations would ordinarily not be included here, there are occasions when students are selected or encouraged to give a presentation because of superior performance in class or because they have done research on a topic that is being studied in class. In those instances, such experiences should be listed. If you want to highlight significant presentations, you might consider establishing a separate category for them.

Preliminary Version

Edited for Revised Version

Edited for Final Version

Work Experience

In this section, list all of your work experiences, including internships, volunteer work, summer jobs, and work on campus, and give brief but complete descriptions of your responsibilities. Use action verbs to describe your responsibilities. (See appendix B for a selected list of action verbs.)

Provide your title(s), the name and location of the organization or business, and when you worked there. There is no particular order in which this information might be presented. You should, however, present it in the order of importance you deem appropriate. If, for example, you want to emphasize your job titles, then they should be positioned at the beginning of an entry. However, if you want to emphasize the organization or business where you worked or volunteered, *that* information should be presented at the beginning of an entry. Do not include the address or telephone number of an organization or business where you were employed.

If your supervisor enjoys wide recognition in her or his profession, it would be appropriate to provide that information. If you are seeking admission to a graduate program in a scientific area that requires clinical and/or work experience that was supervised by a certified professional, you must provide the name and certification of the supervisor. For example, if an applicant seeking admission to a graduate program in clinical psychology has some clinical experience that was supervised, the clinical supervisor should be identified and that information should be included in the entry.

To ensure comprehensive description of all of your experiences, discuss each item with your academic adviser or the director of the career planning center at your college or university.

Preliminary Version

Edited for Revised Version

Edited for Final Version

Professional Associations/Learned/ Scientific Societies

Membership in organizations such as the American Chemical Society, the Modern Language Association, the American Psychological Association, and the Mathematical Association of America, should be listed here. If you have not obtained membership or some sort of affiliation with a professional, learned, or scientific society of the discipline in which you plan to pursue graduate study or seek a position, you should do so as soon as you become eligible for membership. Such affiliation or lack thereof can be interpreted as an indication of the level of enthusiasm you have for your intended areas or fields of study.

There are other advantages of belonging to professional organizations. For example, they publish scholarly journals and literature on major issues in their fields of interest. They also convene conferences that provide opportunities for interaction with other scholars, frequently on a national and international level. Furthermore, they are generally a rich source of information regarding opportunities for job placement within their fields.

You will find a selected list of major U.S. and Canadian professional, learned, and scientific societies in appendix C.

Preliminary Version

Edited for Revised Version

Edited for Final Version

Background

This category anticipates the section on graduate and professional school applications where applicants are asked to provide additional background information that might not have been requested in other sections of an application. This category might include information regarding citizenship, prolonged residence abroad, and/or unusual educational or work experiences. Do not include information that alludes to race, ethnicity, religion, gender, age, or political preference.

Preliminary Version

Edited for Revised Version

Edited for Final Version

Community Service

This category includes community responsibilities and/or university-wide committee memberships. There might be some overlap for undergraduates between this category and co-curricular activities.

Preliminary Version

Edited for Revised Version

Edited for Final Version

Cocurricular Activities

List and describe campus programs and activities in which you have been an active participant.

Preliminary Version

Edited for Revised Version

Edited for Final Version

Interests

This category includes avocations. List them even though such items might appear in other contexts throughout the CV.

Preliminary Version

Edited for Revised Version

Edited for Final Version

Travel

This category is designed to include travel—usually international travel. Brief visits to countries as a tourist should not be included. If you have had extensive domestic travel that is related to your objective(s), it should be mentioned. When appropriate, list cities, states, regions, or countries alphabetically with descriptions of experiences and length of visits.

Preliminary Version

Edited for Revised Version

Edited for Final Version

References/ Recommendations

List only the names and titles of individuals you have asked to write recommendations for you. This category is entirely optional. Since most institutions maintain a placement file for students, requests for recommendations are generally referred to undergraduate institutions or the institution of your most recent attendance. If appropriate, you may simply indicate the following on your CV:

Placement credentials available from
NAME OF INSTITUTION AND APPROPRIATE OFFICE
OR
References available upon request

Should you decide to list the names and addresses of individuals who will write recommendations for you, be certain that they are willing to be contacted without direct communication from you. To guard against unauthorized requests, you should have clear operational guidelines with persons writing recommendations.

Preliminary Version

Edited for Revised Version

Edited for Final Version

≡ 5 ≡
The Final Draft

POLISHING YOUR WORK

Thus far attention has been focused on the content of your vitae without regard to such matters as perspective, writing style, grammar, format, and layout. To be effective, your CV must not only be informative but also aesthetically pleasing. This chapter provides some guidelines that will assist you in making some decisions regarding the physical rendering of your CV.

Perspective

The curriculum vitae is used to communicate with colleagues who share a common vocabulary and knowledge of a particular discipline. It is essential that you describe your experiences in language appropriate to your discipline. Also, this is not the time to be modest—be your own advocate!

Writing Style

Display a confident, authoritative, and crisp writing style throughout your CV. (See Appendix D for a selected bibliography of style books and manuals.) Be concise, economical, and consistent in content and format. Use telegraphic style. Avoid the use of first person singular pronouns. Use definite articles selectively.

Grammar

Grammar and spelling must be perfect. Use tenses that are always in agreement with occurrences of actions. Use parallel grammatical phrases.

Computer Assistance

Because of the pervasive use of computers in all aspects of our academic and professional lives, you should use one to prepare your vitae. It is the most effective and highly efficient means of producing, revising, and storing the information for your CV.

Laser printers make the best copies. Choose a font size and style that is conservative, attractive, and easy to read.

Postal Abbreviations

Use U.S. and Canadian codes: for example, for New York, NY; for Pennsylvania, PA; for Ontario, ON; and for Quebec, PQ. Be consistent in this usage throughout your CV. (See appendix A for U.S. and Canadian postal abbreviations.)

Spacing, Underlining, Capitalization

Double or triple space between categories; single space within. Allow appropriate indentation with liberal use of white space. To highlight information, use underlining, capitalization, and boldface type for variety and emphasis. If you use full capitalization, do not underline.

Paper

Use 20-pound, $8^{1}/_{2}'' \times 11''$ bond paper to produce your CVs and accompanying correspondence. Should you decide to use colored paper, use a conservative, light color, such as off-white, light beige, blue, or gray. White paper with black ink, however, works extremely well.

Professional Printing

Obtain assistance from professional printers in producing multiple copies of your CV. It is your responsibility, however, to verify the accuracy of their work.

Length

Avoid lengthy descriptions of academic and work experiences. Descriptions of six lines or more are difficult to scan and thus should be avoided.

If the final draft of your CV comprises more than one page, type your name and the appropriate page number on each successive page. Your CV ideally should not be more than three pages in length. While there is no collective agreement regarding the appropriate length of a vitae, it is nonetheless essential to know that only the *truly* extraordinary individual is able to maintain enthusiasm for his or her background beyond three pages. If, however, your CV moves beyond that, speak with your academic adviser or mentor about it. Should you have a lengthy list of publications, presentations, performances, exhibitions, or awards, use addenda or attachments to your CV to describe them. Doing so can eliminate the need to include this information in the CV itself and will give the reader the option of perusing this information.

Proofreading and Revisions

Proofread and revise each draft of your CV. At this stage, you should only work from final drafts because you will need to proofread and revise the content and review the draft from the perspective of each item in this chapter.

Critique(s)

Ask several colleagues to critique a draft of your vitae. You should also request a similar critique from your academic adviser or mentor. Recognize that you might not agree with some or all of the critiques that this process will generate. Therefore, it is essential that you are able to justify to your own satisfaction the content and format of your CV.

Copies

Make a hard copy of the final draft of your CV and accompanying correspondence and keep a file of them. Update your CV every year or as frequently as you have new information to add to it.

≡ 6 ≡
What to Send with Your Curriculum Vitae

Objectives of the Cover Letter

A well-written letter satisfies the following objectives:

- It offers the job seeker an opportunity to personalize and target the résumé [curriculum vitae] to a particular person

- It allows the writer to direct particular attention to specific skills that may be important to the reader

- It enables the applicant to clearly state why this organization is of interest to him or her

- It opens the door for further communication and follow-through

---

Adapted from *The Resume Handbook*, by Arthur D. Rosenberg and David V. Hizer, Holbrook, MA: Bob Adams, Inc., 1990.

Effective correspondence with individuals and organizations that might advance your achievement of career or vocational goals is an essential ingredient in the application or job search process. While the correspondence that accompanies a curriculum vitae is generally referred to as a *cover letter*, it is in fact defined, shaped, and determined by its diverse purposes. There are, for example, letters of application, inquiry, rejection, acceptance, referral, withdrawal, to name but a few. What you will send during the application or job search will depend entirely upon your needs.

The essential structure and format of the correspondence adhere to some commonly agreed upon guidelines even though there is wide flexibility regarding important matters of content, tone, style, and focus. While you are naturally expected to exercise prudent judgment in these matters, your primary consideration must always be the production of prose of the highest and most inspired quality.

Write with clarity, persuasion, honesty, and economy. You cannot afford to do otherwise. Grammar, rhetorical style, format, even punctuation and appearance, require the same focused attention that you give your curriculum vitae, since this correspondence speaks for you at the most important stage of your application or job search—that initial stage when decisions are made that will determine whether you receive an interview or remain in the pool of applications that do not survive the paring process.

Cover Letter Guidelines

The Secrets to Success in Cover Letters
- Relevance
- Appropriateness
- Clarity
- Brevity
- Sincerity and warmth
- Uniqueness

1. Address your letter to someone who has authority to hire you or to have an impact on your admission (or acceptance). Use that person's name and title.

2. Find out as much as you can about the organization from which you are seeking employment (or admission).

3. Sound enthusiastic and interested.

4. Be professional, warm, and friendly.

5. Set yourself apart from the crowd. Identify at least one thing about you that is unique—something that distinguishes you and that is relevant to the position or program for which you are applying.

6. Be specific about what you are asking for and what you are offering.

7. Be brief.

Adapted from *Resume Pro: The Professional's Guide*, by Yana Parker. Berkeley, CA: Ten Speed Press, 1993.

GUIDELINES FOR EFFECTIVE CORRESPONDENCE

1. Eric Martin and Karyn Longhorne provide creative information and exercises that describe the process of self-assessment—a systematic evaluation of your

strengths, interests, and personal style, which is a critical preliminary step before you prepare your correspondence. They also provide useful information that will help you determine what you need to know about the individuals and organizations to whom you direct your correspondence.[1]

2. Effective communication involves shared understandings. Enhance the quality of your communication by using keywords and phrases about yourself, as well as information from your profession or discipline, an advertisement, information you glean from descriptive pamphlets, brochures or films, and any other information that will show that you have a clear understanding of yourself and have carefully researched the organizations or individuals with whom you must now communicate.

3. It is essential that the tone of the correspondence accurately reflect the tenor of the messages you want to convey. Be certain that your language and the format of your correspondence reflect such positive characteristics as career maturity, enthusiasm, intelligence, creativity, energy, organization, attention to detail, and skills appropriate to your focused interest.

4. In some cultures, especially in academia, it is sometimes considered "bad form" to view or even use accompanying correspondence, CVs, and other accoutrements of the application or job search process as marketing tools. While it is quite understandable that marketing oneself might clash with the values of some individuals, it is nonetheless naive to assume that it is not part of the process of competition for positions. It follows then that each individual will need to assess his or her values and decide the extent to which this correspondence will be an effective marketing tool.

5. Richard Beatty insists that correspondence should generally be written so that it is directly related to the way it will likely be read.[2] This approach naturally shifts the focus away from correspondence that is focused on the writer and towards the needs of the individual or organization for which it is intended. As a vehicle for transmitting vital information about your accomplishments, skills, and background appropriate to your objectives, effective correspondence must find congruence, explicit and, even in some cases, implicit with the needs of a prospective employer or the expectations of an admission officer or sponsor of a research grant. This requires an astute ability to read between the lines in an effort to target effectively your correspondence. The between-the-lines information represents the nuances that are often not stated but which are often *inferred* by an individual. The classic example of

1. Martin, Eric R. and Karyn E. Longhorne. *How To Write Successful Cover Letters*. Lincolnwood, IL: VGM Career Horizons, 1994.
2. Beatty, Richard H. *The Perfect Cover Letter*. New York: John Wiley & Sons, 1989.

such a situation is the individual who applies for a position that has clearly defined specifications, but who is offered another position because his or her unique talents surface during the course of effective correspondence. While this is not a common occurrence, it is nonetheless an eventuality that resourceful individuals create for themselves.

6. Correspondence should generally be restricted to one page. This is not an inflexible guideline, however, as there are occasions when it is appropriate or even expected that correspondence will exceed one page. Correspondence regarding grant applications or communication with professional associations and learned societies are examples of occasions when you must focus on the content of the communication rather than on some arbitrary rule regarding length.

7. Address the following:
   - Detailed information specific to the purpose of your correspondence (e.g., the date you will begin employment, your response to salary and benefits packages; or information regarding individuals who have agreed to write letters of recommendation)

   - Appropriate and specific information describing your education and work background, skills, interest, publications, presentations—in short, highlights from your CV that should generate enthusiasm in the reader for more detailed information about you, and

   - Actions you will take following that communication

Cover Letter Ingredients: A Basic Checklist

For letters to be effective, they must:

- Address a person, not a title . . . and wherever possible, a person who is in a position to make a hiring decision
- Be tailored to the reader as far as is practical, to show that you have done your homework
- Show concern, interest, and pride for your profession; demonstrate energy and enthusiasm
- Cut to the chase
- Avoid stuffiness, and maintain a balance between professionalism and friendliness
- Include information relevant to the job you are seeking
- Ask for the next step in the process clearly and without either apology or arrogance

---

Adapted from *Cover Letters that Knock 'em Dead*, by Martin Yate. Holbrook, MA: Bob Adams, Inc., 1992.

Preparing Final Copies of Correspondence

1. Since a growing number of organizations store information on disks, prepare your correspondence so that it can be easily scanned, that is, produced by a computer with a letter-quality printer that is equipped with print styles and fonts appropriate to this technology. The same guidelines apply for preparing correspondence.

2. Choose a style or format and remain consistent in its use throughout your correspondence.

3. Should you decide to have your correspondence prepared by a professional typesetter, remember that the entire letter must be prepared that way. While this is an option for some, the letter quality laser printed correspondence is entirely appropriate since it can and often does rival professionally typeset material.

4. Always proofread your correspondence several times before mailing it. The perils of failure to do so—misspellings, typographical errors, errors in grammar, and ineffective style and format—far outweigh the extra time and energy involved.

In the remainder of this chapter we will look at several sample letters that will assist you in preparing effective accompanying correspondence.

Acceptance Letter

February 1, 19_____

Ms. Marianne Meadows
Commissioner
Kentucky State Board of Tourism
Capital Plaza Tower
500 Mero Street
Frankfort, KY 40601

Dear Ms. Meadows:

I am writing to inform you of my acceptance of your offer to become the director of the Kentucky State Board of Tourism effective February 4, 1996. Pursuant to the contract I have signed, I shall report for work at 10:00 a.m. on the above mentioned date.

Please know that I remain enthusiastic about the development of tourism in the great state of Kentucky. The broad economic returns that can accrue to the residents of the state are certainly powerful incentives for vigorous and imaginative implementation of tourism programs.

I am eager to join my colleagues in this important endeavor. Thank you again.

Sincerely yours,

Davin P. McCormick
7 Kellogg Circle
Kalamazoo, MI 49032-3160

Enclosure: Contract

Full Block Style

Response to An Advertisement Letter

2 Fisherman's Cove
San Francisco, CA 94682
1 February 19_____

Dr. Alva Marie Demetriades
Senior Vice President
The JohnstonWells Group
720 Writer Square
1512 Larimer Street
Denver, CO 80202

Dear Dr. Demetriades:

I am applying for the position of research associate at The JohnstonWells Group. The description of the position, as advertised in *The San Francisco Chronicle*, is congruent with my educational and work background in health care public relations. Having written speeches and researched the mechanics of the health care system for senior executives of health management organizations, public and private hospitals, physicians' consulting groups, etc., I have acquired the high degree of expertise in analytical and communication skills that define the position with you. Moreover, my facility with state-of-the-art computer assisted research in biotechnology augment those skills.

I have enclosed a portfolio of samples of my writing along with a recent copy of my curriculum vitae. As this is a confidential search, I would appreciate an opportunity to speak with you concerning individuals whom I might approach for references. You can appreciate, I am certain, the delicacy of interlocking relationships in the highly interconnected field of health care public relations.

Congratulations on receiving the International Public Relations Award for research on marketing support of health care providers. It is a fine tribute to the quality of the service offered by The JohnstonWells Group. I shall contact you regarding my response to your advertisement in three weeks. Should you need to contact me before that time, please call my 24-hour answering service at 415/555-6874.

Thank you.

Sincerely,

Omo J. Kacendar

Enclosures (2)

Modified Block Style

Application Letter

14 Overland Street
Youngstown, OH 33602-1110
15 October 19_____

His Excellency S. K. Ghusayni
Embassy of Lebanon
2560 28th Street, NW
Washington, DC 20008

Excellency:

I am applying for the position of Assistant Professor of English at American University of Beirut. Since the position, which was advertised in the *Chronicle of Higher Education*, requires some teaching at Université Saint Joseph, I am sending a set of my credentials to you and representatives of the respective institutions. This is a particularly exciting position as I would be able to use my knowledge of Arabic and French, which would enhance the effectiveness of my English language instruction.

As my enclosed curriculum vitae indicates, I received a Ph.D., *magna cum laude*, with a major in English and Linguistics, from Yale University in 1994. Prior to that, I obtained a B.A., *magna cum laude*, in French and an M.A., *summa cum laude*, in French Literature from the Massachusetts Institute of Technology. During my Fulbright Scholarship for study of French literature at the Sorbonne, I read extensively the works of writers from Algeria, Tunis, Martinque, and other Francophone countries.

The paramount experience that has influenced my decision to apply for this position, however, was a three-year teaching position at Mohammed V University in Morocco. Not only did I teach English but I also developed an innovative program in Arabic using computer assisted pedagogy. It was recognized as a major breakthrough in Arabic language instruction.

I plan to be in Washington, DC, during the week of 18 February and would like to arrange an interview with you at your convenience. I will telephone you next week to arrange that meeting. Please feel free to call me at 216/555-8209 or by fax at 216/555-8210.

Thank you for your consideration. I remain

Yours truly,

Zoltan M. Zantovsky

Enclosures: Curriculum Vitae
             Book Reviews
             Disk Containing Arabic Language Course
             Letters of Recommendation

Modified Block Style

Continuing Interest Letter

P.O. Box 1872
Santa Fe, NM 87492
7 June 19_____

Mr. Joseph Jackson
Editor
The Plain Dealer
1801 Superior Avenue
Cleveland, OH 44114-2037

Dear Mr. Jackson:

I am writing to inform you of my continuing interest in the position of Associate Sports Editor of *The Plain Dealer*. Your forthright expressions of confidence in my journalistic skills and publication background convinced me that I would grow and mature as a sports editor in the demanding yet supportive culture at *The Plain Dealer*.

You will be pleased to know that eager and ofttimes perplexed sports fans in Santa Fe read with interest the continuing negotiations among the Cleveland Browns, the City of Cleveland, and the National Football League. Needless to say, I am enormously impressed by *The Plain Dealer's* in-depth coverage of all aspects of the momentous decisions that confront all of the players in this pivotal episode in professional football. Of course, the Cleveland Indians cast a wide enough shadow of winning respectability for the other professional teams to find at least a brief moment of pause and comfort.

A very interesting thing happened to me on my return to Santa Fe. I met, purely by chance, Mr. Michael Doerfler, a retired gentleman who was a sports columnist for *The Plain Dealer*. Let me assure you that he had some great stories to tell about milestones in professional sports in Cleveland. He regaled me with accounts of personal encounters with individuals from all levels of that segment of society. I am eager to become a part of that hallowed tradition.

Thank you again for your generous hospitality during my recent visit.

Sincerely,

Strobe L. Watson II

Modified Block Style

Declination Letter

September 25, 19_____

His Excellency Livingston Gomez Gotaz
Embassy of the Republic of Cote D'Ivoire
2424 Massachusetts Avenue, N.W.
Washington, DC 20008

Dear Dr. Gotaz:

Thank you for offering me the position of assistant to the cultural attaché for graduate education. Unfortunately, I received your cablegram several weeks after I had accepted a similar position with another country and thus must decline your offer.

I am, however, encouraged by your continuing interest and support of the graduate studies of your students in the United States of America and expect that we will continue to have occasions to discuss our mutual interests in international education.

Thank you again for your kindness during my interview and in subsequent conversations with you. Please accept my standing invitation for tea when I am next in Washington, DC.

With best regards,

Aiesha Sente-Mendoza
10-107 Magnolia Boulevard
Baton Rouge, LA 70666-0005

Full Block Style

Networking with Friends Letter

Theta Kappa Psi Fraternity
University of Connecticut
203 Broad Street
Storrs, CT 06269-1008
March 25, 19_____

Jed Aaron Smith, Jr.
Executive Secretary
Theta Kappa Psi Fraternity
University of Utah
Boulevard of the Americans
Salt Lake City, UT 84202-7600

Dear Jed:

Greetings from the cold, windswept tundra of Storrs, Connecticut, and its only bright spot this weekend of weekends! With several hundred graduating seniors of TKP from twelve schools in the northeast due on our campus tomorrow, we should have a great career fair. It was great seeing you and all the brothers at our alumni officers' gathering at the University of Florida. I tell you, the warm weather makes me seriously think of transferring there.

Just wanted to get off a quick note to you to let you know that I am indeed interested in the new position of Executive Secretary for Alumni Affairs at our national headquarters at Indiana University. Although I would prefer an assignment at the University of Florida or the University of Texas, I could live with Indiana University, particularly when it would involve such extensive contact with all of our chapters throughout the United States. I would greatly appreciate a good word from you to the search committee on my behalf. In fact, I plan to call Jim at UCLA and Bob at UNLV and take them up on their offer to intercede on my behalf.

All of this feels just right! With TKP growing in all parts of the country, our alumni will be assuming increasingly important responsibilities in the overall management of each of our chapters.

Take care and have a great time on the slopes. See you at the University of Colorado next month, TKP just do it!

Fraternally yours,

Jared Angier Solomon
Alumni Secretary

Enclosure: Curriculum Vitae

cc: James M. Braithwaite
    UCLA

    Robert S. Pendergast
    UNLV

Full Block Style

Prospecting Letter

January 29, 19_____

Ms. Daphne Lizbet Middlemiss
Photographic Director
ARTnews
40 West 38th Street
New York, NY 10000-2222

Dear Ms. Middlemiss:

Cats! I love them! You love them! Your recent photographic features on Egyptian cats at court and Siamese cats in Thai arts were riveting and captivating works of artistic expression. For that reason and the obvious cachet that your publication enjoys in photography and art, I have decided to apply for a staff photographer position at ARTnews.

It is fitting that I have made this decision after being informed by *National Geographic Magazine* that my set of photographs of Bengal tigers and a diary associated with each shooting will appear in its Fall 1996 issue. That exposure and the recognition I am receiving for my exhibition of photographs of the flora and fauna along the Amazon River support my strong interest in a position with you.

I have enclosed a copy of my curriculum vitae and a set of slides, which describe the diversity of my photographic techniques, the equipment, and the materials I use in producing them.

Should you plan to attend the Art in Urban Landscape Biennial in Baltimore on March 30, 1996, I would like to speak with you about my interest in joining the staff of ARTnews. I will contact you in two weeks to arrange a meeting. Since I travel frequently, I am always in touch with my 24-hour answering service (804/555-6635). Please leave messages for me there.

Thank you for the wonderful photographs of cats. Muffin, my beautiful, moody, sensitive, bright, black and white cat, is peering at me from her exalted position in the middle of my desk. Does she know what I am doing?

Take care!

Cordially,

David (Shenandoah) Runningbear
25-10 Orchard Park
Charlottesville, VA 22391

Full Block Style

> Referral Letter

July 20, 19_____

Dr. Hillary Theakston
Department of Psycholinguistics
Bloomfield Hall
University of Pennsylvania
Philadelphia, PA 19104-6226

Dear Mr. Theakston:

Dr. Anton P. Cleggart, Matthew J. Owens Professor of Linguistics at the University of Delaware, suggested that I contact you regarding postdoctoral fellowships in psycholinguistics at the University of Pennsylvania. Since you have had a long and distinguished career in this field, he even suggested that I approach you regarding the prospect of obtaining a fellowship under your supervision.

I am very enthusiastic about the prospect of continuing my research on the psychological impact of autism on language acquisition in preverbal four-year-old children. Your paper at the recent annual meeting of the American Psychological Association further stimulated my interest in working with you.

I have enclosed a copy of my curriculum vitae along with a letter of introduction from Dr. Cleggart. Please contact me by E-mail so that we may arrange a time to talk about my proposal.

Thank you for your consideration.

Sincerely,

Dr. Siobhan Y. Kaufman
University of Delaware
Department of Psychology
Spruce Hall
Newark, DE 19617
E-mail:siobhan.@psych.edu.

Enclosures: curriculum vitae

cc: Dr. Anton P. Cleggart

> Modified Block Style

Search Firm Letter

1472 Rockland Estate
Hanover, NH 03744
August 8, 19____

Dr. Danielle Linton-Panko
President
Panko, Linton, Jawarski, Paolone & Associates
Research Triangle Park
Building 16-62
Durham, NC 24720-0001

Dear Dr. Linton-Panko:

Your article, "An Analysis of Einstein's 1905 Specialty Relativity Paper and Its Implications for Pedagogy in Technical Writing," which appeared in the *Journal of Technical Writing and Communication* (volume 25, Number 1, 1995), is extraordinary research whose outcomes will have far reaching implications for pedagogy in technical writing and communication. It has therefore made imminent sense for me to contact your firm, as I now begin my search for a teaching position in technical writing. Its highly regarded profile in this field, coupled with your reputation for placement success, made the choice of your firm inevitable.

I have enclosed a copy of my curriculum vitae, which describes my educational and work background. After a decade of quality experience at IBM and Argonne National Laboratory in hardware and software documentation, on-line documentation, research in writing, and technical journalism, I am now seeking a teaching position at a major research university or laboratory in the Boston area.

In addition to articles in the *New York Times, The Washington Post,* the *Los Angeles Times,* and the *Chicago Tribune,* I am now a syndicated technical/scientific columnist with Gannet Newspapers and Associated Press. My most recent publication is the second edition of my book, *Technical Documentation On the Internet*.

Dr. Danielle Linton-Panko
Page 2

I am eager to speak with you about procedures for becoming a client with your firm.
Please fax the appropriate information to me at the address above, or contact me by E-mail
at mpp@anl.com.

Thank you for your consideration, and I shall look forward to hearing from you. This
inquiry should be kept confidential.

Sincerely yours,

Marva Pallante-Pezzenti

Enclosures (2)

Full Block Style

Targeted Letter

Ishmael Benjamin Herera
Department of Mechanical Engineering
University of Mississippi
Cobalt Hall, Room W
University, MS 38323

December 12, 19_____

Nissan of North America
Attention Environmental Compliance Officer
1000 Lake Shore Drive, Suite 900
Detroit, MI 48200-3222

Attention: Environmental Compliance Officer

In the November/December 1992 issue of Environmental Waste Management, it was reported that Nissan of North America "leads major auto companies in the United States by making air conditioning systems free of ozone-depleting CFCs available in nearly two-thirds of the 1993 models it manufactures." As a doctoral student in automotive/mechanical engineering at the University of Mississippi, I have followed closely the continuing efforts of automobile manufacturers to comply with environmental regulations of this type. Your firm's success has attracted the attention of researchers here at the University of Mississippi.

I am therefore writing to you in an attempt to arrange a summer internship at Nissan of North America, which would provide me with access to data that details the results of your efforts in reducing ozone depletion.

If it is appropriate for me to work with you on this proposal or contact someone else at Nissan, I would be pleased to do so. I will contact you next week regarding the next steps in the process of arranging this internship. Please contact me at the Department of Mechanical Engineering, University of Mississippi at ishmael__herera@olemiss.ums.edu.

Thank you.

Sincerely,

Ishmael Benjamin Herera

Full Block Style

Thank You Letter

May 5, 19_____

The Honorable Svetlana Teraskova
Member of City Council
County Court House
The City of Lake Forest
Lake Forest, IL 60012

Dear Councilwoman Teraskova:

Please accept my appreciation for arranging my attendance at the extended meeting of the City Council of Lake Forest, Illinois, last month. As a result of that experience and my extensive conversation with you, I have decided to continue my graduate studies in urban affairs and will focus those studies on the gentrification of Chicago's northside neighborhoods.

Again, I want to thank you for expressing your enthusiasm for my studies and for the opportunity to discuss some of my ideas with you and your colleagues.

Sincerely,

Qian Xinzhong
16 Seventh Avenue
Topeka, KS 32130

cc: Mr. Abraham Troutmeyer
     Chair
     City Council
     The City of Lake Forest

Modified Block Style

Withdrawal Letter

October 24, 19____

Mr. Nicholas Y. Spurgeon
Vice President for Human Resources
Toys "R" Us, Inc.
461 From Road
Paramus, NJ 07652

Dear Mr. Spurgeon:

I am writing to inform you that I am withdrawing my application for the position of Vice President for International Marketing. As you know, the sharp fluctuations in the securities market have enhanced the value of the dollar, thus affecting favorably my current position. This has reinforced my decision, which we discussed at length as one of the several options available to me, to remain here. In short, that is what I will do.

Thank you for spending your very valuable time with me at each critical juncture of this decision. I am certain we will have occasions to share ideas regarding effective international marketing of toys as we vigorously pursue international markets for our products.

Enjoy your upcoming trip to Singapore.

Cordially,

Roberto Juan Castillo
9440 Lehigh Parkway
Fort Myers, FL 33711-6200

Modified Block Style

≡ 7 ≡
Distributing Your Curriculum Vitae

The effective distribution of your curriculum vitae and accompanying correspondence is as important as the quality of the material itself. It requires a comparable degree of creativity, thoroughness, and attention to detail in order to achieve the desired results. It is therefore essential to view the process of distribution as an important means of marketing yourself—that is, bringing information about yourself to the attention of individuals or organizations.

To be effective in your overall marketing effort, you need strategies that are consistent with your personality and the degree of comfort you feel about presenting yourself for evaluation. For example, a reticent person should not use the same strategy as a gregarious individual who has strong interpersonal skills and who is interested in projecting that image.

A marketing or distributional strategy for your CV should include the following elements.

Congruence

Maintain congruence between your professional, career, or vocational goals and your marketing strategy. While diverse objectives require diverse strategies, it is essential, at this stage, to be certain that the information on your CV complements your objectives.

Research

Use the research approaches and skills you have developed and honed through your academic experiences to obtain information about individuals and/or organizations you plan to contact. The quality of this research will naturally affect the approach and the information you include in your correspondence, the negotiation strategies you use in obtaining and conducting interviews, and the general outcomes of the complete process. Know as much as you can about the intended recipients of your correspondence.

Self-Management

You need to manage the marketing and distribution of your correspondence as well as all other aspects of your application process or job search. This means you must give careful attention to such matters as time management, record keeping, follow-up, and negotiation strategies. Know where you are in every step of the process and exercise control over each element to assure desired outcomes.

Self-management can be one of the most nettlesome aspects of this emerging marketing and distributional strategy. Although some of the psychological issues involved in preparing a CV have been addressed in chapter 1, it is instructive to review some issues regarding management style.

The worst time to seek a position is when you do not have one and must get one. The pressure to obtain a position can lead to the production of an inadequate CV and marketing strategy that reflects necessity rather than opportunity. Likewise, an impending application deadline can cause panic in some individuals and thus result in a less than outstanding effort.

Other individuals, however, are actually energized by impending unemployment or application deadlines and, in effect, do their best work under pressure. In fact, in some circles it is a badge of honor of sorts to do things at the last minute. Whatever your management style, know its possibilities and limitations. Structure and manage the marketing and distribution strategy accordingly.

Distribution Checklist

This checklist will facilitate the effective distribution of your correspondence. Modify and adapt it to your needs.

1. _____ Enclose a curriculum vitae with applications to graduate and professional programs. Provide all the information that is requested on an application. Refer to your enclosed CV, however, when inadequate space is available for the information that is requested, or when you are instructed or encouraged to provide additional sheets for such information.

2. _____ Enclose a curriculum vitae and accompanying letter with applications for grants, fellowships, and scholarships, even though they

may not be required. An attractive CV can enhance an application and therefore should always be enclosed unless it is strictly forbidden by a fellowship, grant, or scholarship sponsor.

3. _____ Submit a CV and letter when requesting information regarding a position that an organization has not advertised. Enclosing a CV with the letter of inquiry precludes the necessity for follow-up correspondence to request it.

4. _____ Submit a CV and letter with employment applications or responses to advertised positions.

5. _____ Cultivate the art of preparing lists, writing brief notes, and keeping logs on targets of your marketing/distributional process. Prepare lists of prospective recipients and rank them in order of importance to you. Also, keep track of all correspondence, as this information will assist you in maintaining effective follow-up.

6. _____ Keep the number of organizations and individuals you contact within manageable limits. While the distribution of a large number of CVs might engender feelings of accomplishment, the effective follow-up that is required might become impossible or at least difficult to manage. You might mail information at different times so that responses will follow at different intervals.

8
Sample Curricula Vitae

The experiences of fictitious individuals described in the sample CVs provide concrete examples of content, style, and format that will assist you in devising the presentation of your own unique experiences.

Undergraduate
African American Literature
Art
Chemistry
English
Geology
Neuroscience
Political Science

Graduate
Anthropology
Astronomy
Clinical Psychology
Computer Science
Economics
German
Mathematics
Women's Studies

Professional
Architecture
Business
Engineering
General Medicine
Law

African American Literature

Curriculum Vitae

JUDE WESLEY GREEN

26 River Road	Box 928, Bowdoin College
Bainbridge, GA 31728	Brunswick, ME 04011
(912) 555-3973	(207) 555-0922

PROFESSIONAL OBJECTIVE

Ph.D. in African American Studies

RESEARCH OBJECTIVE

To develop psycholinguistic profiles through study of autobiographical narratives of ex-slaves of African descent in eighteenth, nineteenth and twentieth century America.

EDUCATION

1996 B.A.   **Bowdoin College**, Brunswick, ME.

Major in Afro-American Studies (GPA 3.7); minor in psychology (GPA 3.7) and computer science (GPA 3.6). Cumulative GPA 3.7.

Candidate for high honors in Afro-American Studies.

1994–1995   **Tougaloo College**, Tougaloo, MS.
Studied linguistics, music and anthropology.

Summer 1995   **Yale University**, New Haven, CT.
Studied psycholinguistics, African American literature of the Colonial Period, and computer applications for research in the humanities.

COURSEWORK

Afro-American Studies
African-American History
The African Diaspora
Race and Ethnicity
African-American Fiction
Africa and the Slave Trade

Psychology
Introduction to Psychology
Developmental Psychology
Personality
Language: A Developmental
 Perspective

JUDE WESLEY GREEN
Page 2

COURSEWORK
(continued)

Computer Science
Introduction to Computing II
Computer Organization
Principles of Programming Languages
Theory of Computation

Other
Swahili
Survey of American Literature
Printmaking
Forms of Narrative

HONORS AND AWARDS

Phi Beta Kappa, Alpha of Maine. Bowdoin College, 1996.

Dean's Award, seven of seven semesters. Bowdoin College.

Abraxas Award for highest standing during first year. Bowdoin College.

The George Duane Kimbrough Prize for Academic Excellence in Computer Science. Bowdoin College. 1995

The Adam Clayton Powell Scholarship for Excellence in Afro-American Studies. Bowdoin College. 1995

SKILLS

Academic: Strong problem-solving, critical judgment, conceptualization, and research skills; comfortable in unstructured academic environments where initiative and creativity are encouraged.

Languages: Conversant in Latin; proficient in reading Swahili and French.

Computer:
Word Processing: Word Perfect 5.1
Microsoft Word 5.0

Spreadsheet: Lotus 1–2–3
Quattro Pro
Quattro

Programming: Pascal, C, (dBase III for AIX)

Hardware: IBM RISC System 600, PS2, RT, AT

AFFILIATIONS

National Urban League

Association for the Study of Afro-American Life and History

JUDE WESLEY GREEN
Page 3

EXPERIENCE

Coach, Junior Tennis Teams, Hutto High School, Bainbridge, GA. Summer 1994.

Recreation Assistant/Counselor, City of Bainbridge Parks and Recreation Program, Bainbridge, GA. Summer 1993.

Research Assistant, Dean of Students Office, Bowdoin College. Wrote computer program for housing lottery. 1994.

Student Representative, Board of Proctors, Bowdoin College. 1993–1995.

INTERESTS

Spirituals, philately, tennis, swimming.

Art

PHOEBE A. PARKER _____

_____ Box 207, Beloit College, WI 53511, (608) 555-2761

77 Cypress Way, Palm Beach, FL 29073, (305) 555-1596 _____

PROFESSIONAL OBJECTIVE

Independent artist supported by exhibitions and publications

A R T   S H O W S

- Spring 1996   One person show of environmental sculptures and landscape paintings—series of seascapes emphasizing play of light on water with contrasting water pollutants in staged relief

- Fall 1995   Wright Museum of Art, Beloit College. Series of self-portraits dealing with emotional responses to test anxiety.

- Summer 1995   Crispen Gallery, Palm Beach, FL. Series of oil paintings of children visiting a planetarium

- Spring 1995   Notten Gallery of Art, Philadelphia, PA. One-person show of watercolors of artists at work.

- Fall 1994   The Gallery of the Department of Art and Art History, Beloit College. Series of photographic images of players in Virginia Slims Tennis Tournament.

W O R K - I N - P R O G R E S S

Photographic images of blossoming dandelions (Independent Study)

Portraits of growth stages of children through adolescence

- Dean's Award (GPA 3.3)
  Six of six semesters

- Senior Bench Chapter of
  Mortar Board, 1996

- Shirley Stewart Foster
  Scholarship for
  Excellence in Studio Art,
  1995

- American Pewter Guild

- Surface Design Association

- Wisconsin Women Sculptors

- Women's Caucus for Art

HONORS

AFFILIATIONS

Beloit College   Beloit, WI

B.A., May 1996

Major: Art and Art History (GPA 3.5)

Minor: Museum Studies (GPA 3.2)

Cumulative GPA 3.3

Candidate for honors in Studio Art

The Art Institute   Chicago, IL

Summer 1995.   Studied sculpture

EDUCATION

PHOEBE A. PARKER   page 2

Model

Department of Art
and Art History
(Studio Art),
Beloit College.
1995–1996

Model and Writer

Blackstone Photographic
Modeling Agency.
Minneapolis, MN. 1995

Costume Designer

University Theatre
productions of
*Barefoot in the Park,
A Funny Thing
Happened on the Way
to the Forum,*
and *Evita.* 1995–1996

E X P E R I E N C E

Docent

Wright Museum
of Art,
Beloit College.
1996

Intern

Museum of Modern
Art, New York, NY.
Catalogued acquisitions
in Eskimo art collection.
Summer 1995

Apprentice

Pierre L. Lovin,
environmental
sculptor
Madison, WI.
1994–1995

Art and Art History

Basic Studio
Drawing I, II
Painting I, II
Sculpture I, II

Photography I, II
Ceramics
Art History Survey I
Senior Seminar in Art
  and History

C O U R S E W O R K

Communication Arts

Stage Management
Scene Design
Costume Design
Arts Management

Related

British Literature I, II
Shakespeare
Psychology
Images of Modern Man
Astronomy

PHOEBE A. PARKER   page 3

Chemistry

CLEMENTINE OPHELIA HARE

2 Quackenbush Lane
Tuscaloosa, AL 34586
(205) 555-5660

Box TU 6071 Newcomb College
New Orleans, LA 70118
(504) 555-2777

PROFESSIONAL/CAREER/RESEARCH OBJECTIVE

A research position that requires background in organic synthesis and/or chemical identification through spectrographic techniques such as NMR, GC, IR, UV-Vis and mass spectroscopy.

EDUCATION

B.S., 1996, Newcomb College of Tulane University, New Orleans, LA. Major in chemistry, GPA 3.3; cumulative GPA 3.2.

1993–1994, University of Tennessee, Knoxville, TN.

Summer, 1992, University of Alabama, Tuscaloosa, AL. Studied biochemistry and environmental geology.

COURSEWORK

(*denotes courses taken at University of Tennessee)

Introductory Chemistry I*, II*
Organic Chemistry I*, II*, III
Advanced Organic Chemistry
Physical Chemistry I, II
Advanced Inorganic Chemistry
Independent Research in Chemistry
Senior Research in Chemistry

Instrumental Methods
Calculus I*, II
Physics I, II
Biology I*, II*
Environmental Hazards
Natural Hazards
Environmental Geology and Natural Resources

Related courses: Intermediate Louisiana French
Cajun Art and Music of the Nineteenth Century
Roots of Western Civilization
The Modern Experience in the West
Mass Media, Mass Society and the Individual

LABORATORY EXPERIENCE

Research Assistant. Chemistry Department, Newcomb College.
Under Dr. M. P. Norris, Spring 1996–Fall 1996.
Experimented with synthesis of B-amino ketones via enol boronates, as they pertain to natural products.

Research Assistant, Chemistry Department, Newcomb College.
Under Dr. M. P. Norris, 1995–1996.
Experimented with SmI selective bond cleavage of carbon-oxygen single bonds.

Research Assistant, Chemistry Department, University of Tennessee.
Under Dr. Craig Barnes, Summer 1994.
Synthesis of macro-cycle containing two transition metal atoms.

Research Assistant, Chemistry Department, University of Tennessee.
Under Dr. Craig Barnes, Spring 1994, Fall 1994.
Synthesis of starting material for graduate student research.

CLEMENTINE OPHELIA HARE
page 2

INSTRUMENTATION EXPERIENCE

(1) Nuclear Magnetic Resonance
(2) Infrared and Ramen Spectroscopy
(3) Ultraviolet and Visible Absorption Spectroscopy
(4) Mass Spectrometry
(5) Atomic Absorption Spectrometry
(6) High Performance Liquid Chromatography
(7) Gas Chromatography
(8) Fluorimetry
(9) Gel Electrophoresis

MEMBERSHIP

Younger Chemists, American Chemical Society, 1996.

HONORS AND ACHIEVEMENTS

Haskell-Schiff Memorial Prize in chemistry for outstanding performance in first year chemistry, 1992.

Allen Mathematics Prize for excellence in Calculus II.

Captain, National Championship Swim Team, 1991.

All-America, High School swimming, 1990, 1991.

Athletic Scholarship (swimming), University of Tennessee, 1992–1994.

COCURRICULAR ACTIVITIES

Varsity Swim Team, Tulane University, 1994–1996.

Varsity Swim Team, University of Tennessee, 1993–1994.

Big Brother/Big Sister, Newcomb College of Tulane University, 1994–1996.

Tutor, Chemistry Department, Newcomb College of Tulane University, Fall, 1995. Assisted students in Advanced Organic Chemistry.

OTHER EXPERIENCE

Assistant to the Manager, Welsch Electric Co., Tuscaloosa, AL.
    Coordinated warehouse inventory with showroom inventory. Summer 1996.

Coach, Tuscaloosa Swim Club, Tuscaloosa, AL. Summer 1995.

Coach, United Swimming Clinics, Mercersburg, PA. Summers 1993, 1994.

English
curriculum vitae

phillip hogarth hedgeworth
- box CDE, colgate station, hamilton, new york. telephone (315) 555-1234
- 4 stanton place, rochester, new york. telephone (716) 555-4569.

---

literary interests

continued work in writing and poetry, focusing on the development of craft, image, and voice; study of psychological and cultural complexities of poems and poets; interest in works of pound, williams, lowell, bishop, plath, hayden, ginsberg, and rich.

---

workshops

poetry writing workshop—professor bruce berlind
emphasized critique and discussion of form and content. experimented with syllable verse, sestinas, and various other rhyme and metrical schemes.

short fiction workshop—visiting author david bradley
emphasized extensive revision of working short stories. four drafts written over course of three months. mr. bradley stressed combination of creativity and discipline.

independent in reading and writing poetry—professor bruce berlind
a month-long intensive study of modern poets such as richard wilbur, denise levertov, and ted hughes. also wrote and revised two or three poems per week and met with professor berlind for discussion sessions.

---

cocurricular activities

co-founder, colgate university poetry society, 1995. organized and participated in poetry workshops every other week. edited and published poetry in *the colgate maroon*.

co-founder and assistant president, colgate literary society, 1995–1996.
organized bureaucracy to tie literary aspects of the colgate campus together. ran poetry and short fiction workshops. organized faculty lectures and co-sponsored visiting writers. administered the first in a series of poetry, short fiction and essay contests. hosted informal group discussions on literary topics.

poetry editor, the colgate maroon, spring, 1996. one of two colgate weekly newspapers.

editor, the pallette and the pen, colgate's literary and art magazine, fall 1995.
contributed poetry spring 1995, fall 1995, and spring 1996.

member, amnesty international, colgate chapter, 1994–1996.

member, students for environmental awareness, 1995.

---

education

b.a., may 1996, colgate university, hamilton, new york
major: english, gpa 3.7
workshop, gpa 3.7
minor: history, gpa 3.4
cumulative gpa 3.4

phillip hogarth hedgeworth
page 2

---

coursework

---

english
workshops
poetry—professor berlind
*poetry—professor
 balakian
short fiction
independent—reading and
 writing poetry
other
british literature I
british literature II
american literature
the novel I
the american novel
shakespeare
literature of the 17th
 century
*the brontes

history
growth of nation-states
 in europe
europe in crisis since
 1815
u.s. in vietnam (1945–75)
formation of the russian
 empire
history of american
 diplomacy
*seminar: problems in
 american diplomacy
cultural identity of
 europe

related
roots of western
 civilization
the modern experience
north american indians
international ethics
*ethics
*mass media, society,
 and the individual
introduction to religion
the buddhist tradition
comparative cultures
contract tradition in
 modern thought

*denotes spring 1996 courses

---

honors

---

dean's award for academic excellence; six of six semesters

edward wood scholarship 1995, academic excellence

allen poetry award 1996, literary excellence

runner-up, colgate winter poetry contest 1993

honorable mention, colgate literary society fall 1995 poetry contest

honorable mention, world of poetry national poetry contest summer 1994

selected member, colgate geneva study group fall 1994. traveled throughout western europe. studied various international organizations in depth.

---

other experiences

---

lifeguard, athletic department, colgate university, 1993–1995.

student worker, case library, colgate university, 1994–1996.

carpenter's assistant, alternative timber structures, summers 1993–1995
 richard g. smith, contractor, summer 1995
 robert g. rose, contractor, january 1993

lifeguard, marriot hotel, henrietta, new york, summer 1994.

Geology

MARIA VALESQUEZ COLON_____

(permanent)   (until 20 June 1996)
2733 Willow Park Drive   University of Rhode Island, Box 8028
Golden, CO 80401   Kingston, RI 02881
(303) 555-9822   (401) 555-0630

EDUCATION   B.A., June 1996, University of Rhode Island, Kingston, RI.
                Major in geology (GPA 3.4) with primary interest in oceanography.
                Cumulative GPA 3.3.

COURSEWORK

<u>Geology</u>	<u>Related Sciences</u>
Physical Geology	Chemical Principles I
Oceanography	Chemical Principles II
Mineralogy	Calculus I
Petrology	Computer Science II
Coastal Geology	Physics I
Structural Geology	Physics II
Marine Geology	
Stratigraphy and Sedimentation	
Invertebrate Paleontology	
Applied Field Geology	

<u>Other</u>

Economic Principles
Introduction to Philosophy
Psychology
Intermediate Portuguese
Political Science
History of Egypt
American Education
Mass Media

HONORS   Dean's Award, six of six semesters
             Phi Eta Sigma, honor society for first-year students, 1993.
             Recipient, The Camille and Henry Dreyfus Foundation Scholarship for National Merit Finalist
                 studying chemistry or related sciences.

SPECIAL SKILLS

Language: Fluent in Spanish; conversant in French and Portuguese
Computer: Languages: Ada, APL, C, Modula II, PROLOG, PL/I, SNOBOL, FORTRAN, and COBOL.
            Hardware: Apple IIE, Macintosh, SE Plus, IBM PS2, IBM 5291 models 1 and 2.

Maria Valesquez Colon
page 2

LABORATORY EXPERIENCE

Researcher: The Sediment History of the Pettaquamscutt River and its Relation to the Narragansett Bay, RI. Dr. J. King, advisor. Fall 1994.

Research Assistant, Lake Ontario Coastal Survey, Colgate University, Department of Geology. Dr. C. McClennen and Dr. P. Pinet, advisors. Fall 1995.

Research Fellow, University of Rhode Island, Graduate School of Oceanography, Narragansett, RI. The Sediment History of Heavy Metal Pollution in the Pettaquamscutt River, RI. Dr. J. King, advisor. Summer 1994.

Research Assistant, United States Geological Survey, Branch of Atlantic Marine Geology, Woods Hole, MA. Lake Michigan Lake Level Study: performed grain size analysis on cores. Dr. S. Coleman, Advisor. January 1995.

Researcher, Coastal Geomorphology, cuspidal beach formations and their relation to rip currents. Dr. C. McClennen, advisor. Spring 1995.

Teaching Assistant, Mineralogy, University of Rhode Island, Department of Geology. Dr. J. Novacek, Instructor. Fall 1994.

INSTRUMENT EXPERIENCE

- Coulter Counter/Elzone
- Freeze Drier
- X.R.F.
- Rock Saw
- S.E.M.
- I.C.P.
- Piston Corer
- Shatter Box
- X.R.D.
- Freeze Corer
- Smith-McIntyre Grab
- Cryogenic Magnetometer

OTHER EXPERIENCE

Tour Guide, Enviro Tours, Everglades, FL. Conducted environmental tours of Central America. Summer 1995.

COCURRICULAR

- *Certified*, NAUI Openwater I SCUBA diver.
- Position #1, Women's Cross-Country Ski Team, 1993–present.
    Captain, 1992.
- Latin American Student Association, 1993–present.
- Pi Beta Phi Fraternity for Women, 1994–present.
- Cycling Team, 1995.
- Geology Club, 1993–present.

TRAVEL

Extensively throughout Spain, Portugal, Finland, Sweden, Denmark, and Norway; resided in Oslo, Norway for two years (1991–1993).

Neuroscience

SARAH RUTH EISENBAUM*

P.O. Box 92, Brandeis Station
Waltham, MA 02254
617-555-8677

7 Evergreen Court
Highland Park, IL 60031
708-555-9081

RESEARCH OBJECTIVES

Neural plasticity in the mammalian CNS, i.e. the capacity of brain cells to change as a function of experience or environmental demand; field properties of the retina during synaptic drug application.

      Long range: M.D. – Ph.D.

EDUCATION

    B.A., cum laude, June 1996. Brandeis University, Waltham, MA.
       Major in neuroscience (GPA 3.5); minor in Judaic Studies.
       Cumulative GPA 3.6.
       High honors in neuroscience.

    Summer 1995, Columbia University, New York, NY.
       Studied psychological measurement and applications of experimental
       psychology.

    Spring 1993, Swarthmore College, Swarthmore, PA.
       Studied Hebrew (intermediate level), modern Hebrew literature,
       comparative psychology, and genetics.

COURSEWORK

Neuroscience

Introduction to Neuroscience
Inorganic Chemistry I, II
Organic Chemistry I, II
Genetics
Cellular Biology
Functional Neuroanatomy
Clinical Neuroanatomy
Fundamentals of Neurochemistry/neuropharmacology
Fundamentals of Neurophysiology
Neural Cell Culture
Senior Thesis I, II

Psychology

Experimental Psychology
Quantitative Methods
Comparative Psychology
Physiological Psychology
Personality

Judaic Studies

Religion and Literature of the Old
  Testament: Through the
    Babylonian Exile
Classical Judaism

Intermediate Hebrew
Modern Hebrew Literature
Texts and Images of the
  Holocaust

SARAH RUTH EISENBAUM
page 2

COURSEWORK (continued)

<u>Other</u>
Calculus III
Physics I, II
The American Novel
British Literature

RESEARCH EXPERIENCE

Senior Thesis. "The Afferent Gastric Vagal Fibers are Critical in Food Related Drinking in Rats."
Program in Neuroscience, Department of Psychology, Brandeis University. Thesis Advisor,
E. L. Baum, Ph.D., 1995–1996.
Examined the effect of selective vagotomy of both the anterior and posterior gastric trunks,
selective vagal afferent denervation with capsaicin, and selective vagal efferent
blockade with atropine on drinking caused by eating in rats.

Research Assistant. Bonney Center for the Neurobiology of Learning and Memory, University of
California, Irvine. Summer 1994.
Supervisor Dr. James L. Lee. Received NSF Grant.
Examined role of specific nuclei of the amygdaloid complex involved in the amnestic effects
produced by benzodiazepines in rats; observed role of nucleus of the solitary tract as
a possible relay station between the peripheral nervous system in aversive memory
formation in rats.

Research Assistant. Department of Anatomy and Cellular Biology, University of Illinois,
Champaign–Urbana. Summer 1993.
Supervisor Dr. Lois M. Rogers.
Examined nerve growth factors receptors of chick and quail embryos using *in situ*
hybridization and autoradiographic techniques.

SPECIFIC SKILLS

Surgery (rat)

—Stereotaxic cannulae and electrode implantation
—Lesioning, electrolytic as well as chemical via microinjections with Hamilton syringe
—Full anterior and posterior trunk vagotomies including selective vagal denervation using
capsaicin
—Gastric fistula implantation

SARAH RUTH EISENBAUM
page 3

SPECIFIC SKILLS (continued)

Histology

—Perfusion with saline and formalin.
—Tissue sectioning using freezing microtome and Cryostat
—Microscope slide subbing and mounting of tissue on slides
—Lesion verification using projector and microscope

Staining

—Cell body (Cresyl violet)
—Direct immunofluorescence
—Indirect immunoperoxidase
—Autoradiography

Behavioral Training/Testing

—Radial arm maze
—Inhibitory Avoidance (IA)
—Continual multiple-trial IA
—Water maze
—Y-maze

Cell Culture

—Aseptic technique
—Preparation of primary cultures of Schwann cells from rat sciatic nerve
—Preparation of mixed cultures of oligodendrocytes and astrocytes from neonatal rat brain
—Staining techniques mentioned above

INSTRUMENTATION EXPERIENCE
(1) Cell Culture —sterile and aseptic technique
—media preparation
—maintenance and preparation of primary cultures: Schwann cells, Astrocytes
—cell lines; PC12, B49, B50
—transfected Schwann cells—SV40

(2) Molecular Biology —plaque lifting screening
—immunological screening of a cDNA library
—isolation of mRNA
—Northern Blotting
—manipulation of plasmid vectors using restriction enzymes
—preparation and assay of bacteriophase lysates
—determination of concentration of cultures by
    antibody titer
—plasmid DNA purification

SARAH RUTH EISENBAUM
page 4

INSTRUMENTATION EXPERIENCE (continued)

    (3) Biochemistry —Western Blotting
                      —SDS-PAGE electrophoresis
                      —Silver Straining
                      —electro-elution
                      —scanning densitometry
                      —Lowry Protein Assay
                      —cell fractionation
                      —Differential Centrifugation
                      —gradient gels
                      —Ultraviolet/Visual Spectroscopy
                      —Enzyme Linked Immunosorbent Assay

    (4) Biology —Transmission Electron Microscopy
                  —Scanning Electron Microscopy
                  —Nissl Staining
                  —Audioradiography

COMMUNITY SERVICE

Volunteer, Department of Psychological Services, Brigham and Women's Hospital, Boston, MA.
    Supervisor: Dr. Dawne Allette-Noel, specialist in study of Alzheimer's disease. 1994.

Volunteer, Neurobiology Division, The Massachusetts Mental Health Center, Boston, MA
    Supervisor: Dr. Sander Gorham. 1995.
        Counseled patients in early stages of Parkinson's Disease.

Circulation Assistant, Gerstenzang Science Library, Brandeis University. 1993–1994.

    *Information contained in the categories RESEARCH EXPERIENCE and SPECIFIC SKILLS is from the curriculum vitae of Dean Michael Cestari '92, Colgate University, neuroscience major. The information in the category INSTRUMENTATION EXPERIENCE is from the curriculum vitae of Lisa Petronella '92, Colgate University, neuroscience major. This information is used with their permission.

Political Science

Curriculum Vitae

YOKO I. NAKAGAWA

Box 903 College Station, Norman, OK 73069   (405) 555-2187

6 Jackson Way, Seattle, WA 98100   (206) 555-4563

BACKGROUND

Dual Japanese/Canadian citizenship with permanent residence in the United States. Past residence in the Netherlands and Canada. Fluent in Japanese; conversant in Dutch.

EDUCATION

B.S., June 1996. University of Oklahoma, Norman, OK. Major in political science; minor in geography. Cumulative GPA 3.5. Candidate for high honors in political science.

RESEARCH INTERESTS

The nature of concept formation and theory construction in political science with particular emphasis on utopian impulses in political philosophy.

COURSEWORK

Political Science

Introductory I
Comparative European Politics
American Political System
National Institutions and the Policy Process
Parties in the Political Process
European Security and Integration
National Security
Family in Political Thought
Living Politicians: The Electoral Process

Geography

Human Geography
Political Geography
Geography of Development: Asia
Environmental Geography
Environmental Issues
Environmental Hazards
Environmental Impact Assessment

Related

Calculus I
Elementary Russian I, II
Oceanography
Introductory Economics
Living Writers
Modern Philosophy

Aquatic Insects
Chinese Studies
World Food and Hunger
Comparative Cultures
Social and Political Ethics

YOKO I. NAKAGAWA

HONORS

Pi Sigma Alpha, national political science honorary society.

Dean's Award (3.3 GPA). Five of six semesters.

Member, American University London Study Group. Studied political and economic policies of European community. Achieved 3.7 GPA. Spring 1993.

Colonel J. G. McCoy Scholarship. Wrote paper, ''China: A Ten Year Prediction.'' Received $3,000. 1993.

Research Assistant to Mary Margaret McShane, Ph.D., Distinguished Professor of Political Institutions, The Carl Albert Congressional Research and Study Center, the University of Oklahoma. Analyzed document of funding sources of independent political parties for Dr. McShane's book, *Political Action in the 80's: Americans Outside of the Political Mainstream*. 1996.

EXPERIENCE

Kappa Kappa Kappa Sorority. 1993–present.

> *Steward*. Administered budget of $52,000. Directed preparation of all meals; organized modernization of kitchen facilities; supervised five student workers and cook. Fall 1994.

> *Social Manager.* Administered budget of $16,000. Spring 1995.

> *Scholarship Chairperson*. Organized tutoring program; originated sorority computer center. Fall 1995.

> *Member*. Sorority Executive Committee. 1995–present.

Intern, Daiwa Securities Co., London, England.
Assisted head trader of United Kingdom Equities Division in product research; observed trading procedures of London Stock Exchange. Spring 1993.

Intern, Nikko Securities Co., New York, NY.
Aided in assembling daily trade information for brokers; planned study program of the New York Stock Exchange for Nikko interns. Summer 1994.

Intern, United States Senator Alphone D'Amato (R–NY), Washington, DC.
Aided legislative assistant in researching legislation and reporting on committee hearings. Gained familiarity with structure of Capitol Hill and Senate offices. January 1995.

Volunteer, Saracens Rugby Club, London, England.
Assisted in coaching and managing rugby team for girls ages ten through twelve. Spring 1993.

COCURRICULAR

Representative. Student Affairs Board. 1993–1994.

President's Committee on Investments. 1995.

Asian Society. 1994–present.

SKILLS

Conversant with political issues at all levels of government; practical experience in problem-solving; excellent oral and written communication skills.

Anthropology

NGOZI AWOJOBI **Curriculum Vitae**

BACKGROUND   Nigerian citizen with permanent residency in the United States of America; extended residency in England, Canada, and Barbados; fluent in Igbo, Swahili, Yoruba, English, and French; advanced knowledge of computer systems and applications in social science research.

President	THE NGAMI MFUMBIRO FOUNDATION Lagos, Nigeria and Washington, DC	1992–present

Manage a by-invitation coterie of African, Middle Eastern, and Near Eastern countries which support economic, educational and scientific development in their respective countries; supervise staff of 75 consultants in Lagos office and 200 in Washington; manage annual budget of $50 million; report to Board of Advisors comprised of representatives of participating countries and funding areas.

October–February
2107 R Street, NW
Washington, DC 20009
202/555-3187 (tel)
202/555-3189 (fax)

March–September
PMB 1209, Sijuada
Lagos, Nigeria
(1) 6120789 (tel)
28763 (telex)
(1) 6120663 (fax)

WWW:http://www.nawojobi

Ngozi Awojobi   **page two**

Accomplishments

- Increased endowment from $120 million to $180 million in four years

- Increased awards, grants, scholarships, fellowships by fifty percent in four years

- Expanded scope of scientific grants to include telecommunications and aerospace engineering

- Developed innovative program for recruiting expatriate scholars for positions at universities and research institutions in the home countries

- Actively established cooperative projects with other international foundations with similar interests

- Organized and managed development staff that continually seeks innovative sources of funding for foundation projects

---

SUMMARY OF QUALIFICATIONS

- Dedicated to efforts to improve the quality of life of all people, especially those in Africa, the Near East, and Middle East

- Successful in bringing diverse opinions and ideas to consensus

- Innovative thinker and problem-solver

- Excellent communication and persuasion skills

- Conceives, develops, and implements creative programs targeted for special populations.

Ngozi Awojobi   **page three**

EDUCATION   HARVARD UNIVERSITY, Cambridge, MA

Ph.D., anthropology, *summa cum laude*   1985

Major: cultural anthropology

Dissertation, awarded High Honors: "The development of anthropological writing as it has
         moved through culture critique: the use of knowledge of other cultures to examine the
         assumptions of our own"

Areas of specialization:
- Socio-economic transformation of indigenous societies and their transition to market
  economies
- Transformation of indigenous local organisations into development organisations

Research interests:
- Symbolic analyses of women and rituals in Igbo culture
- Ethnic formation and transformation—the Arolgbo ethno-history

AHMADU BELLO UNIVERSITY, Zaria, Nigeria

M.A., cultural anthropology, African History (Honours)   1982

Thesis: "Comparative analyses of kinship, marriage, and family in matrilocal societies in
        Nigeria"

UNIVERSITY OF IBADAN, Ibadan, Nigeria

B.A., geography and mathematics, Honours   1978

HONORS   Senior Fulbright Scholar-in-Residence, SUNY Farmingdale
  and
AWARDS   International Fellow, American Association of University Women Award for dissertation

            Research Fellow, Rockefeller Foundation, Ahmadu Bello University

            Faculty Prize for Best Graduating Student, Ahmadu Bello University

Ngozi Awojobi **page four**

RESEARCH
EXPERIENCE

FORD FOUNDATION, Lagos, Nigeria 1991
Trained and monitored 300 rural women to enhance development potential of
their indigenous association; formed Abo Umulolo Women's Cooperative as
forum for installing motorised engines for cracking palm kernels and milling
maze, beans, and cassava

UNICEF, Imo, Nigeria. Research Consultant 1990
Monitored and evaluated impact of participatory approach to Rural Drinking
Water Supply and Sanitation Project.

ROCKEFELLER FOUNDATION, Lagos, Nigeria 1990
Used anthropological and historical theories and methods, especially oral
traditions, in study of the Aro of southeastern Nigeria.

TEACHING
EXPERIENCE

HARVARD UNIVERSITY, Cambridge, MA. Teaching Fellow 1992
Courses taught:
—Film and Anthropology: The Translation of Culture
—Economic Anthropology

BOSTON COLLEGE, Chestnut Hill, MA. Assistant Professor 1991
Courses taught:
—Economic Anthropology
—Race and Society

UNIVERSITY OF NIGERIA, Nsukka. Professor, Department Chair 1990
Courses taught:
—Anthropological Theories
—Marxist Sociology
—Rural Development Studies
—Systems of Social Inequality
—Women and Development

PUBLICATIONS

Awojobi, Ngozi. *The Aro of Southeastern Nigeria*. Ibodan,
Nigeria: University of Nigeria Press, 1994.

_____. *Economic Anthropology*. Washington: Smithsonian Institution
Press, 1994.

_____. "Women in African Society," in The Place of Igbo Women in Igbo
Culture. *Nigerian Journal of Economic and Social Studies* 50 (1990),
pp. 38–72.

Ngozi Awojobi   **page five**

PUBLICATIONS (continued)

Awojobi, Ngozi and Catherine E. Shu. ''Cultural Ecology of Agrarian Societies,''
in *Contemporary Readings in Sociology*. Chicago: University of Chicago
Press, 1992.
Awojobi, Ngozi and Joi Chin. ''Ethnology of the Near East and North Africa,''
in *Signs* 85 (1989), pp. 56–66.

AFFILIATIONS

Association of African Women for Research and Development (AWARD)
Association of American Anthropologists
Nigerian Association of Sociologists and Anthropologists
Nigerian Economic Society
Nigerian Academy of Science
Nigerian Institute of International Affairs

BOARDS

Social Science Research Council
Society for Applied Anthropology

Astronomy

Curriculum Vitae   **AARON J. LEVY**

residence: 3 Rosebud Terrace   office: 4800 Oak Grove Drive
          Pasadena, CA 91102   Pasadena, CA 91109
          (818) 555-9079   (818) 555-6583
          Fax: (818) 555-9090   Fax: (818) 555-9854

EDUCATION

Ph.D., UNIVERSITY OF WASHINGTON   Seattle, WA
                                                                              1992

        Major: astronomy
           Research interests: radio astronomy; optics; x-ray observations, stellar evolution

B.A., *magna cum laude*, REED COLLEGE   Portland, OR
                                                                               1985

        Major: astronomy
        Minor: classics

RESEARCH INTERESTS

Optics; radio astronomy; stellar astronomy; extragalactic supernovae; optical systems and design; CCD photometry of extragalactic supernovae.

EXPERIENCE

JET PROPULSION LABORATORY   Pasadena, CA
        California Institute of Technology   1995–present

        Associate Research Astronomer

           Research interests: adaptive optics; charge-coupled devices; infrared dector
                                  arrays; interplanetary optical communications;
                                  telecommunication systems; artificial intelligence

           Manage $500,000 budget; supervise four post-doctoral research fellows, two Ph.D. candidates, and eight undergraduate assistants.

page 2   **AARON J. LEVY**

EXPERIENCE
(continued)

UNIVERSITY OF CALIFORNIA, BERKELEY   Berkeley, CA
                                                                          1993–1995

Adjunct Assistant Professor of Astronomy

Research and instructional interests:
    circumsteller molecular envelopes of evolved stars; luminous hot stars (type O
    and B, and the Wolf-Rayet stars); x-ray extreme ultraviolet and far ultraviolet
    observations of evolved stars; joint projects with Laboratoire d' Astronomie
    Spatiale in Marseilles, France.

UNIVERSITY OF FLORIDA   Gainesville, FL
                                                                          1992–1993

Post-doctoral Research Associate

Research interests: radio astronomy; dynamical and solar
                     system astronomy; stellar evolution.

UNIVERSITY OF WASHINGTON   Seattle, WA
                                                                          1991–1992

Graduate Research Assistant
    Co-investigative Assistant, Infrared Astronomical Satellite, 1987.

NATIONAL RADIO ASTRONOMY OBSERVATORY   Charlottesville, VA
                                                                          1990

Summer Research Assistant

GEORGIA TECH RESEARCH INSTITUTE   Atlanta, GA
                                                                          1989

Summer Research Assistant

Research interests: infrared/electro-optics; microelectronics; millimeter wave
                     technology.

SPECIAL SKILLS

Computer: Scientific software and hardware development; system modeling; database
           management; mathematical modeling; IBM large-scale systems; UNISYS; and VAX
           computers.

PUBLICATIONS

Journal articles
refereed

A.J. Levy, T.M. Avery, O.L. Braun, "Optical identifications of high luminosity infrared sources," *Astronomical Journal*, 201, 1411–1420 (1991).

A.J. Levy, S.M. Smith, R.A. Quakenbush, "The Hubble Space Telescope: ultraviolet and x-ray observations," *Astrophysical Journal*, 80, 1202–1218 (1993).

Books

A.J. Levy, *Paths to the Present: Origins of Elliptical Galaxies,* John Wiley & Sons, Inc. 225 pp (1992).

A.J. Levy, *Directory of Observatory and Satellite Facilities in the United States and Canada*, John Wiley & Sons, Inc. Vol. I, II. 400 pp. (1993).

Thesis

A.J. Levy, "Instrumentation in radio astronomy," Ph.D. dissertation, University of Washington, 275 pp (1992).

PRESENTATIONS

"Instrumentation in radio astronomy," oral paper, American Astronomical Society Meeting, Princeton, NJ, June 1991.

"An observational study of barium stars and their relation to Cepheids," American Astronomical meeting, Tucson, AZ, 1982.

"Infrared detector arrays," NOAA workshop on "Infrared Emission from Active Galactic Nuclei," Madison, WI, June 1993.

GRANTS

*Interplanetary optical Communications," Arizona Space Grant Consortium, 1992.

> Two year grant of $50,000. Support for travel to
> observatories to conduct astronomical observations,
> student and faculty wages, and equipment.

page 4

AARON J. LEVY

GRANTS
(continued)

"Luminous Hot Stars," National Science Foundation, College Science Instrumentation Program, June 1993.

>Two year grant of $45,000, matched by University of California, Berkeley, for computer system to be used at University of California, Berkeley.

Travel grant of $5,000 from United States National Committee to the IAU to attend the International Astronomical Union General Assembly in Marseilles, France, 1995.

COMMUNITY SERVICE

Member, Ph.D. dissertation committees for T.L. Smith (Astronomy 1990–1992) and A.O. Schwartz (Astrophysics 1991–1993), University of Washington.

Member. Committee on Affiliation Services, Lick Observatory, University of California, Santa Cruz, CA. 1990–present.

Member, University committee on user services, Kitt Peak National Observatory and Dominion Astrophysical Observatory. 1991–present.

PROFESSIONAL AFFILIATIONS

American Astronomical Society, 1987–present
Astronomical Society of California, 1990–present
International Astronomical Union, 1992–present
American Association of Variable Star Observers, 1987–present

Clinical Psychology

ZOË E. SCHMIDT

| home: 2764 Smythe Blvd. | Minneapolis, MN | (612) 555-4683 | Fax (612) 555-8710 |
| office: 1 Miller's Place | Minneapolis, MN | (612) 555-6723 | Fax (612) 555-2689 |

RESEARCH INTERESTS

Performance anxiety (academic and music); music therapy

EDUCATION

1994 **UNIVERSITY OF MICHIGAN**
Ann Arbor, MI
Ph.D., Clinical Psychology
Dissertation: "Assessing test anxiety, stress reduction,
and self-concept maintenance among first semester
National Merit Scholars."

1990 **UNIVERSITY OF MICHIGAN**
Ann Arbor, MI
M.A., Clinical Psychology
Thesis: "Psychophysiological investigation of the effects
of positive personality reinforcements and degrees
of uncertainty among Phi Beta Kappa inductees who
are physics majors."

1987 **ST. OLAF COLLEGE**
Northfield, MN
B.A., *summa cum laude*. psychology: minor: music
Elected to membership in Sigma Xi and Psi Chi

HONORS and AWARDS

1993 Division 29 (Division of Psychotherapy)
Winner, graduate student competition for best paper on
measurement, University of Michigan.

1987 Phi Beta Kappa, St. Olaf College

1986 Psi Chi, St. Olaf College

1986 Thomas J. Watson Fellowship for year of independent research in Bolivia,
Turkey, Bulgaria, and France. Topic: "The Effects of lullabies on relaxation
among autistic teens."

ZOË E. SCHMIDT   Page 2

FELLOWSHIPS

1993   Dissertation Grant, Horace A. Rackham School of Graduate Studies, University of Michigan

1995   Postdoctoral Fellowship in Clinical Psychology, University of Rochester and Eastman School of Music, Rochester, NY.
Focus: "Comparative studies of psychomotor dysfunction in breathing techniques among flautists and oboists."

LICENSES

1994   Licensed Psychologist, State of Minnesota
Licence #200

CLINICAL EXPERIENCE

1993–1994   **UNIVERSITY OF MINNESOTA MENTAL HEALTH CENTER**
Minneapolis, MN
Predoctoral Intern (APA approved)

Researched data on adjustment of first semester national merit scholars under supervision of Dr. Sven Lindstrom.

1990–1992   **UNIVERSITY OF MICHIGAN COUNSELING SERVICES**
Ann Arbor, MI
Half-time Psychology Intern

Supervised two master's level interns in counseling practica; taught counseling methods course and measurements course.

1989–1990   **UNIVERSITY OF MICHIGAN COUNSELING SERVICES**
Ann Arbor, MI
Half-time Psychology Intern

Conducted psychotherapy with graduate students pursuing degrees in music; performed psychological consultations and evaluations of anorexic clients under supervision of Dr. Hope Wilson Webber, Clinical Psychologist.

1989   **YPSILANTI PSYCHIATRIC CENTER**
Ypsilanti, MI
Half-time Psychology Intern

Performed psychodiagnostic assessments under supervision of Dr. Agnes Y. Kimbrough, Clinical Psychologist.

ZOË E. SCHMIDT   Page 3

**CLINICAL
EXPERIENCE** (continued)

    1992   **NORTHFIELD SYMPHONY ORCHESTRA**
                  Northfield, MN
                  Crisis Counselor

                    Provided crisis phone counseling and referral
                    information to performers and staff of Orchestra.

    1992   **WALK-IN WOMEN'S COUNSELING CENTER**
                  Northfield, MN
                  Counselor

                    Provided crisis intervention and short-term counseling
                    to single mothers.

**PROFESSIONAL
AFFILIATIONS**

                  American Psychological Association, Division 29
                  Minnesota Women Psychologists
                  Society for Music Therapists

**PUBLICATIONS
and
PRESENTATIONS**

    Allen B., Weinstein, F., Schmidt, Z. (1993). Effects of stress on creativity among teens
        who achieve perfect scores on SATs. *Educational & Psychological Measurement*,
        100, 1108–1121.

    Davis, M., Schmidt, Z., & Musa, M. (1992, June). *Psychotherapy and High Achievers:
        Research Guidelines*. Included in proceedings at Annual Conference of Minnesota
        Women Psychologists.

    Schmidt, Z., & Cohen, A. (1991, September). *Mood and Memory: Evaluating the
        Psychological Functioning of Child Prodigies*. Paper presented at Symposium on
        Creativity, Psychology Department, Stanford University, Palo Alto, CA.

REFERENCES   Available upon request.

Computer Science

JAMAL MARQUIS MAGBY

4 Oahu Drive • Honolulu, HI 96831-3002
808/555-9000 • 808/555-9022 (fax)
www:http//www.jmmagby

PROFESSIONAL OBJECTIVE	A research position in computer and applied mathematics

COMPUTER
SKILLS

Software Development

Extensive knowledge of C; C++, and COBOL; NonStop SQL; data communications/networking; TCP/IP; X.400; X.25; SNA; OSI; Ethernet/802.3; database and design support software; OLTP; fault tolerant computing; RISC technology; UNIX; POSIX and client/server computer.

Hardware Development

Experienced in design, testing, quality assurance, systems integration, reliability, and field engineering of computer systems and subsystems that include CPUs, memory systems, power supplies, power distribution systems, storage devices (tape disks and optical devices), and storage subsystems (device, power, packaging, and controllers). High speed ECL, CMOS, and RISC technologies, which utilize state-of-the-art CAD and CAE design.

Networks

MVS; VM; VSE; OS/400; VMS; JES2; Netview; VTAM; 3090; ES9000; JCL procedures; Netware; WAN; LAN; 3090.

QUALIFICATIONS

- Expert knowledge of mathematical theories of dynamical systems

- advanced knowledge of the application of computer decision making models in the medical sciences

- full knowledge of software and hardware available for research in the natural sciences

- high value placed on teamwork, flexibility, and quality interpersonal communication

- strong analytical, conceptual, and organizational skills

- prompt in planning and implementing agreed-upon proposals and ideas

Jamal MarQuis Magby page two

EDUCATION
■ Ph.D., 1993, Computing and Computational Mathematics, Stanford University, Stanford, CA

Dissertation: "On randomized versus deterministic computation"

Abstract: A study of the relative power of linear and polynomial randomized time compared with deterministic time.[1]

Related courses:
- Numerical Analysis of Dynamic Systems
- Advanced Numerical Analysis
- Advanced Methods in Matrix Computation
- Numerical Methods for Initial Boundary Problems
- Number Theory
- Artificial Intelligence
- Machine Learning
- Methods of Mathematical Physics

■ B.Sc., 1988, Computer Science and Mathematics, University of Hawaii, Honolulu, HI
GPA 3.9 (4.0)

Honors and Awards:
Alpha Theta Mu, honorary society in computer science
Omicron Delta Psi, honorary society in mathematics
Dean's Award (seven of eight semesters)
NCAA Scholar Athlete in Track (200 and 400 meters)

Related courses:

Mathematics	Computer Science
• Mathematical Logic I, II	• Theory of Computing
• Representation and Memory	• Discrete Structures
• Topology	• Operating Systems
• Real Analysis I, II	• Simulation
• Quantitative Reasoning	• Information Systems
• Theory of Algorithms	• Computer Graphics
• Geometry	• Compiler Design
• Differential Equations	• Artificial Intelligence

---

[1]Karpinski, Marek and Rutger Verbeek. On randomized versus deterministic computation. *Theoretical Computer Science*, **154**, (1996), 23–39.

Jamal MarQuis Magby   page three

PUBLICATIONS

Journal Articles

■ J. M. Magby. "New algorithms for signal processing and analysis"
Journal of Computer and System Sciences **21** (1995) 423–475.

■ _____. "Notes on constructive logic and implications for computer science" *Mathematical Structures in Computer Science* **5** (1994) 162–183.

■ _____. "Numerical solutions of boundary value problems" *Mathematical Structures in Computer Science* **3** (1993) 122–145.

Book

■ Magby, Jamal MarQuis. *Studies in Artificial Intelligence.* 3rd ed. New York: Academia Press, 1992.

RESEARCH EXPERIENCE

■ *Research Assistant*, 1994–1995, Aerospace Division, Rockwell, Seal Beach, CA. Member of team of computer scientists who evaluated test data on the performance of the Space Shuttle Orbiter designed and produced by Rockwell. Results will be used in design of electrical power system for space station.

WORK EXPERIENCE

■ *Research Associate*, 1995–present, Digital Data Processing, Massachusetts Institute of Technology, Lexington, MA. Researched systems for more efficient data reduction and analysis as well as improved algorithms for signal processing and analysis.

■ *Research Associate*, 1992–1994. Visual and Systems Interface, Cirrus Logic©, Fremont, CA. Assisted in research in the development of 2D/3D graphics, video, and power management chips for both desktop and portable PCs.

WORK EXPERIENCE

■ *Consultant*, 1991–1993. Worldwide Information Services (WWIS), Unisys Corporation, Bismark, ND. Advise clients in creative use and application of technology to improve service to customers, enhance their competitive position in their marketplace, and increase their flexibility.

■ *Visiting Assistant Professor*, 1990, Department of Computer Science, University of Hawaii, Honolulu, HI. Taught graduate courses in artificial intelligence, algorithms and theory, constructive logic, and computer graphics.

REFERENCES

Available upon request

Economics

CAXTON A. FABERSHAW, IV _____ *Trade Representative*

Canadian Embassy–Apartado Mexico, D.F.
Tel: 555-2222; FAx: 555-0000

EXPERIENCE

- 1994–present   CANADIAN EMBASSY   1150 Mexico, D.F.

  Trade Representative. Negotiate, interpret, and implement Canadian trade policies and agreements of North American Free Trade Agreement (NAFTA); represent Canada in multilateral trade negotiations with Mexico and continuous countries; prepare proposals for trade agreements that enhance profitability of Canadian trade in the hemisphere; advise Canadian firms of market opportunities in the region; supervise staff of thirty associates.

- 1990–1994   ROYAL BANK OF CANADA   Montréal (Québec) H3C 3A9

  Economist. Multinational Banking Division. Analyzed and prepared annual reports on effectiveness of Investment and Corporate Divisions in delivering financial products to corporations, governments and other major institutions around the world; prepared quarterly forecasts of trends in multinational banking.

- 1989–1990   THE INSTITUTE FOR RESEARCH   Montréal (Québec)
  ON PUBLIC POLICY
  L'Institut de Recherche en Politiques Publiques

  Senior Economic Consultant. Convened monthly focus groups comprised of public and private sector executives in discussions of international trade and its impact on public policy; wrote monthly newsletter, which included economic analyses of policies and recommendations for implementation of innovative research programs; obtained $500,000 Canadian Economic Association grant for research on the impact of free enterprise zones on conservative public policies.

Caxton A. Fabershaw, IV _____ page two

AFFILIATIONS

The Conference Board of Canada
North Atlantic Council
      (Delegation of Canada to North Atlantic Council)
Organization of American States
      (Permanent mission of Canada to the Organizations of American States)
Canadian International Development Agency (CIDA)
British Columbia Chamber of Commerce
Musée d' art contemporian de Montréal

EDUCATION

- 1988   PRINCETON UNIVERSITY   Princeton, NJ (USA)

Postdoctoral studies in international economics

Coursework

Advanced Economic Theory	Econometric Modeling
Econometric Theory I, II	Public Finance
International Monetary Theory	International Trade
Scale Economics and Imperfect Competition	Theory and Policy

Research paper: "Factor Movements and Multinational Corporations"

- 1987   THE UNIVERSITY OF BRITISH COLUMBIA   Vancouver, BC V6T 1Z1

Ph.D. (High Honours) in economics

Major: International Economics
Dissertation: "Case Studies in Output and Price Determination in Open Economies."
Awarded J. Peter Norris Prize for Best Dissertation in International Economies

Courses in Economics

Empirical Research in Economics	Money and Banking
Economic History of Canada	International Economics
Labour Economics	Monetary Theory
International Macroeconomics	Econometric Analysis
Topics in Mathematical Economics	International Trade

Caxton A. Fabershaw, IV _____ page three

AFFILIATIONS

- 1984   THE UNIVERSITY OF CALGARY   Calgary, AB T2N 1N4
  B. Sc. (Honours) in psychology
  Concentration: Experimental Psychology
  Minor: Statistics

SKILLS

Languages: Fluent in oral and written French, Spanish, and Portuguese
            Conversant in oral German

Telecommunications: Knowledge of UNIX; DOS environment; C Language; C++;
            LAN/WAN;
            Communication protocols

Computer Networks: OS/400; WMS; JES2; Netview; VTAM; 3090; ES 9000

Computer: Macintosh System ©7 QuickTime 2.0™

PUBLICATIONS

- C. A. Fabershaw. "Myths and Mysteries of Corporate Debt." *The Economist.* 7947, 50–51, (1996).

- C. A. Fabershaw. "Investors and International Markets: An International Economics Perspective." *Fortune.* 133, 1, 60–63, (1996).

INTERESTS

Aboriginal affairs (treaty negotiations; management services; policy; planning, and research);
Ojibway and Cree culture; archery; chess; calligraphy

Spanish and Portuguese versions of this CV are available upon request.

German

JÜRGEN F. ALTSCHULER

2 Appean Way, East
Bloomington, IN 47426
(812) 555-4001
24-Hour message: (812) 555-4711, ext. 29

office: (812) 555-1080, ext. 92
Fax: (812) 555-1087

BACKGROUND

Dual German/American citizenship with permanent residence in the United States of America. Past residence in Germany and Switzerland.

EDUCATION

STANFORD UNIVERSITY   Palo Alto, CA

Ph.D., 1990. Major: Empires of the Mind: Nineteenth Century German Ideas. Topics in politics, religion, society, and history in the nineteenth century; Heine, Hegel, Schopenhauer, Feuerbach, Marx, Neitzsche, Burkhardt, Freitschke, Rauke, D.F. Strauss, Tonnies, Weber, Freud.

Research Interests: Germanic linguistics and philology; foreign language pedagogy; theory of language; and computer assisted text analysis.

Dissertation, awarded **high honors.** Dissertation Review Committee, College of Arts and Sciences: ''Psycholinguistic analysis of print advertisements for pediatric pharmaceuticals in popular journals, Federal Republic of Germany, 1991–1992.''

WILLIAMS COLLEGE   Williamstown, MA

B.A., *summa cum laude*, 1985.

Major: German

Minor: computer science

Senior Thesis: ''Schiller: Aesthetic Theory and Practice. The nature and function of the artist and the work of art, in Schiller's essays, poetry, and dramas.''

JÜRGEN F. ALTSCHULER   Page 2

HONORS AND AWARDS

Phi Beta Kappa, 1985, Williams College.
Goethe Prize for excellence in German language, 1985, Williams College.

Fellowships

UNIVERSITY OF SOUTHERN CALIFORNIA   Los Angeles, CA

1991 Andrew A. Mellon Postdoctoral Fellowship in the Humanities.

> Research: Theories of knowledge, language and the German Tradition.
> Readings in Kant, Herder, Mauthner, Wittgenstein, Heidegger,
> Habermas, and Apel.

> Taught graduate courses on Wittgenstein and literary criticism.

UNIVERSITÄT MANNHEIM   Mannheim, Federal Republic of Germany

> 1988 Deutscher Akademischer Austauschdienst, short-term research grant.

> Research: Foreign language pedagogy.

EXPERIENCE

INDIANA UNIVERSITY   Bloomington, IN

> 1994 *Assistant Professor of German*, College of Arts and Sciences.

> Taught advanced language courses and special topics in theories and history of language,
> aesthetics, literature, and mythology. Team taught courses on computer assisted text
> analysis.

DEUTSCHE GESELLSCHAFT FUR AUSWÄRTIGE POLITIK E.V.

Bonn, Federal Republic of Germany

1993 *Senior Researcher*. Areas of interest:
- The European Community, progress or decline.
- American foreign policy under change; the Middle East and African Policy of the U.S.
  since Carter.

INTERNATIONAL BUSINESS MACHINES   Frankfort, Federal Republic of Germany

1992 *Consultant*, Office of Communications and Global Markets.

JÜRGEN F. ALTSCHULER   Page 3

SKILLS

Languages:

    German: Fluent (speak, read, write, translate, interpret)
    Italian: Conversationally fluent
    French: Conversationally fluent

Computer:

    Hardware: IBM-PC and compatible, Apple Macintosh, VAX 400

    Programming languages: Ada, Modula-2, Pascal, APL, C++, ML, PROLOG, LISP, PL/1, Fortran, Algol, SNOBOL, SIMULA

    Spread Sheet: Quattro

                Quattro Pro

                Lotus 1–2–3

COMMUNITY SERVICE

Member, Ph.D. dissertation committees for D.K. Badenhausen (German language and literatures—1991) and P.A. Koenig (Germanic linguistics and philology—1996). Indiana University.

Faculty Advisor, Goethe Haus, living-learning residence for graduate students pursuing doctorate degrees in German language, 1994. Indiana University.

PRESENTATIONS

Altschuler, Jürgen F. "Fairy Tales as Literary Genre; historic relevance, types of Märchen from Volksmärchen to Kunetmärchen to the Anti-Märchen." Division on Teaching of Literature, MLA Convention. Atlanta, 28 December 1994.

Altschuler, Jürgen F. "Deutsche Kulturgeschichte." Association of German Nobility in North America, Triennial Meeting. Montreal, 1993.

Altschuler, Jürgen F. and Mueller, Max S. "The German Bildungsroman." German-American Chamber of Commerce, Symposium on "Culture and Enterprise." Chicago, 1992.

AFFILIATIONS

International Association of Teachers of German
Modern Language Association of America
American Philological Association
International Association of German Language and Literatures

Mathematics

SUJATA A. CHATTERJEE

8 Colonial Way—Morristown, NJ 07934   Fax: 201/555-6451   Tel: 201/555-6471

BACKGROUND

Dual Indian and U.S.A. citizenship with extended residency in Sweden. Fluent in English, Hindi, Bengali, and Swedish. Superior skills in applied mathematics with particular emphasis on applications of mathematical and computer models for the development of effective management systems.

EXPERIENCE

AT&T BELL LABORATORIES
Morristown, NJ   1994–present

- *Senior Research Associate.* Manage team of twenty-five assistants in longitudinal study of the impact of short-term memory on effective management of hourly employees.

- *Systems Consultant.* Provided sales support, systems analysis and design, and presale management to ensure solutions by AT&T match customers' systems.

- *Development Engineering Intern.* Assisted senior engineers in developing products and systems, improve processes, and conduct analyses.

TATA INSTITUTE OF FUNDAMENTAL RESEARCH
Bombay, India   1991

- *Assistant to Dr. V. R. Singh, Director.* Conducted research in pure and applied mathematics.

BOSE INSTITUTE
Calcutta, West Bengal   1990

- *Research Assistant* in nuclear physics and solid state physics.

BHABHA ATOMIC RESEARCH CENTRE
Bombay, India   1989

- *Assistant* to committee that studied the development of nuclear energy for peaceful purposes.

Sujata A. Chatterjee
Page Two

EDUCATION

MASSACHUSETTS INSTITUTE OF TECHNOLOGY
Cambridge, MA

Ph.D., 1994, (*cum laude*) in applied mathematics

Dissertation: "Linear partial differential operators in Gevrey spaces"[1]

Coursework:

—Ordinary and Partial Differential Equations   —Groups, Rings and Fields
—Theory of Functions of a Complex Variable   —Ring Theory
—Banach Algebras and Spectral Theory   —Representation Theory
—Unbounded Operations   —Homological Algebra
—Classical Harmonic Analysis   —Abstract Harmonic Analysis
—Transformation Groups

UNIVERSITY OF CALCUTTA, Presidency College
West Bengal

M.Sc., 1990, in applied mathematics

Papers:

—K-theory   —Geometry
—Number theory   —General topology
—Set theory   —Statistics
—Mathematical logic and foundations   —Computer science

B.Sc., 1986, (First Class Honours) in mathematics

Pass subjects: physics and astronomy

SKILLS

Educational and practical knowledge of C; C11, UNIX; MS DOS Windows; networking technologies such as WAN, LAN, SNA, CPUs, JCL procedures; ES 9000; COBOL; PASCAL; X.400; X.25; SNA; OSI; database and design support software.

---

[1]Using Luigi Rodino's publication of the same title (River Edge, NJ: World Scientific Publishing Co., Inc., 1993).

Sujata A. Chatterjee
Page Three

POSTDOCTORAL AWARDS AND STUDIES

The Mittag–Leffler Institute, 1991, Sweden
      Award: 100,000 Swedish crowns
      Studies: mathematical physics

The Hugh Kelly Fellowship at Rhodes University, 1990, Grahamstown, South Africa
      Studied pure and applied mathematics

AFFILIATIONS

Association for Symbolic Logic
Association for Women in Mathematics

PUBLICATIONS

S.A. Chatterjee. *"Ordinary differential equations, partial differential equations, and applied mathematics"* Transactions of the American Mathematical Society, **62** (1994), 172–194.

S.A. Chatterjee and Gifford von Edsel. *"A UNIX tool for software development in determining executive compensation packages"* The Computer Journal **27** (1995), 200–239.

S.A. Chatterjee and Mignon E. Delacroix. *"Linear and multilinear algebra: some matrix theories"* Studies in Applied Mathematics, **95** (1993), 6–18.

GRANTS

An empirical study of the impact of perceived environmental uncertainty and perceived agent effectiveness on the composition of compensation contracts. Research supported by a $50,000 grant from the National Science Foundation.

Some advanced technological and organizational implications for change in human resources management. Research supported by a $60,000 grant from AT&T Bell Laboratories.

Women's Studies

MAMIE FRAMPTON-GREEN

permanent:
1235 Central Ave.
Beaufort, SC 29902
(803) 555-1358
Fax: (803) 555-5902

office:
Congress Way and Main
Beaufort, SC 29902
(803) 555-3957
Fax: (803) 555-3958

PROFESSIONAL OBJECTIVE

Ph.D., 1992, in American History

research interests: Transdisciplinary approaches to health care issues of affluent women in Twentieth Century America: 1970–1990

EDUCATION

M.A., 1987, Women's Studies, University of Wisconsin, Madison, WI.

Thesis: "Oral histories of millionaire widows in Philadelphia, PA, Miami, FL, and Phoenix, AZ."

Coursework

Race Class and Gender
Gender and the Economy
Philosophy and Feminism
Latin-American Women Writers
African American Women Writers
Stratification Sociology

Field Methods in Oral History
Women's Health Issues
Women in American History
Corporate Finance
Accounting

B.A., *cum laude*, 1985, Fisk University, Nashville, TN.
Major in history; minor in natural sciences

Senior thesis: Images of affluent women in Pulitzer Prize winning fiction. 1960–1980.

EXPERIENCE

Director, City of Beaufort, Women's Resource Center, Beaufort, SC.

Manage Center that provides family, personal, and career counseling and public health services to professional women; supervise staff of eight including a clinical psychologist, financial planner, psychiatric social worker, and philosopher; manage budget of $400,000; generate 50% of budget from consultant services to government agencies and businesses. 1992–present.

MAMIE FRAMPTON-GREEN
page 2

EXPERIENCE (continued)

Assistant to Director of Community Relations, Bank of New England, Providence, RI.

> In cooperation with health care providers and insurers, developed community-based health care planning program for middle income single mothers. 1989–1990.

Apprentice, Office of Hospital Administration, Nashville General Hospital, Nashville, TN.

> Assisted in assessing the quality of outpatient services for individuals suffering from acute fatigue syndrome; performed data entry using dBase 3. Summer 1987.

Intern, The Tennessee Historical Society, Nashville, TN.

> Edited catalog for centennial celebration. Summer 1986.

COMMUNITY SERVICE

Student Representative, Curriculum Committee, Women's Studies Department, University of Wisconsin. 1988–1989.

Volunteer, HELP-LINE, Nashville, TN. Provided counseling for troubled teens. 1989.

GRANTS

Recipient, American Friends of Cambridge Visiting Research Fellowship in the Arts, Cambridge University, Newham College, Cambridge, ENGLAND.

> Studied social science research methods, social psychology, and economics. 1990–1991.

Recipient, Alisha Sese Seko Travel Grant to Greece.

> Interviewed wives of prominent government officials. Wrote monograph for social science research course at Cambridge University. 1992.

AFFILIATIONS

> National Women's Economic Alliance
> American Historical Association
> American Sociological Association

MAMIE FRAMPTON-GREEN
page 3

SKILLS

Leadership of groups committed to social change; facilitation of individual efforts toward achieving group objectives; motivating individuals to achieve individual objectives; research; problem-solving; observation of phenomena; making critical judgments.

INTERESTS

Detective fiction; Hepplewhite furniture; bridge; chess

Architecture

Caesar Felipe Rodriquez II _____ **Registered Architect**

261 Bloomfield
Otremont, Québec H2Y 1B6
514-555-2301

office:

11 Metcalf
Montréal, Québec H2Y 1B6
514-555-2796
Fax: 514-555-2783

Objective _____

To obtain a position with a licensed architectural consulting firm with client base in arts and entertainment, health care, higher education, and professional athletics.

Background _____

Dual Canadian/Portuguese citizenship with extensive residency in Sao Paulo, Brazil; Lisbon, Portugal; and Houston, Texas.

Experience _____

1992–present   Rodriquez & Rodriquez, Architects   Montréal, Québec

Partner

- Draft and design multibuilding complexes such as college campuses, residential communities, hospitals and nursing homes, and entertainment centres.

- Supervise staff of five associates.

- Arrange client presentations.

- Assist clients in obtaining construction proposals.

1991–1992   Ministère de L'Environnement   Montréal, Québec

Associate Architect

- Assisted in preparation of architectural documents and drawings.

- Researched municipal building codes and materials.

- Wrote specifications for building materials.

Summers 1990, 1991   Ministère du Tourisme   Québec City, Québec

Assistant Architect

- Developed cost figures for construction and maintenance of facilities.

- Prepared drawings, specifications, and related construction documents for facilities.

Caesar Felipe Rodriquez II _____ 2 _____

Education_____

1992 **MSc A**   Université de Montréal   Montréal, Québec
               Ecole d'Architecture
               Faculté de l'Amenagement

Design thesis (awarded high honours): Schematic design of biosphere
   using alternative sources of energy, materials, and
   construction techniques.

Coursework

- CONCEPTS D'SPACE
- RAPPORTS PERSONNE-SOCIETE-ENVIRONNEMENT
- LE DESIGN DEPUIS 1960
- INTEGRATION DE L'ARCHITECTURE AU MILIEU
- METHODES DE RESTAURATION
- LABORATOIRE D'ARCHITECTURE
- LE LABORATOIRE D'ACOUSTIQUE
- LE LABORATOIRE DE CLIMATOLOGIE ET D'ENERGIE
- LE LABORATOIRE D'INFORMATIQUE

1989 **B Arch**   Université de Laval à Québec   Québec City, Québec
                Ecole d'Architecture

Skills _____

- Fluent in English, Portuguese, and French (oral and written;
     writing proficiency in all three languages)
- Strong background and experience in
  —physical sciences
  —humanities
- Detailed knowledge of and practical experience in design
- Proficient in use of computer assisted design techniques

Professional Associations _____

- Ordre des architectes du Québec
- The Royal Architectural Institute of Canada
- Society for the Study of Architecture in Canada

Portfolio _____

Portfolio, references, and transcripts available upon request.

A French version of this CV is available upon request.

Business

curriculum vitae   JOSEPH GERONIMO GIST
                                                          (Sequoya)

Offices

- 1 World Trade Center   - Villa Roma Ippolito
  Suite 9126   Via Grassi 10
  New York, NY 10004   20122 Milano
      (212) 555-8091   ITALY
  Fax: (212) 555-8937   Tel. 243689

EXPERIENCE

- **CHEROKEE INTERNATIONAL MARKETING, INC.**
  New York, NY and Milan, Italy

  President and *Chief Executive Officer* 1992–present

  - Manage $50,000,000 international marketing firm which specializes in providing services for major manufacturers of consumer products.

  - Firm employs 3,000 worldwide.

  - Increased profits 25% (1994) and 35% (1995).

  - Increased clients by 50% (1993); very effective in creating client loyalty.

  - Board of Directors have approved plan for opening offices in Barcelona, Frankfort, London, and Toronto.

- **PROCTER & GAMBLE**
  Rome, Italy and London, England

  Vice President, Marketing European Division 1988–1992

  - Implemented marketing strategies for detergents, soft drinks, and pharmaceuticals.

  - Managed staff of 125 representing numerous cultural and linguistic backgrounds.

- **COCA-COLA FOODS DIVISION**
  Atlanta, GA and Toronto, Canada

  Assistant Vice President, Sales and Marketing 1984–1988

  - Developed and implemented sales/marketing strategy for emerging international markets.

  - Supervised staff of 200 sales personnel in Toronto.

Skills

- Strong conceptualization, analytical, and interpersonal skills essential for administration of an international corporation;

- Proven success in motivating colleagues and staff, and promoting teamwork;

- Significant experience and expertise in developing and implementing sales and marketing strategies particularly for international markets;

- Fluent in Italian, Spanish and German.

Education

- NORTHWESTERN UNIVERSITY, Evanston, IL   1982–1984
  M.B.A. The J.L. Kellogg Graduate School of Management
  Specialty: international marketing

Coursework

- International Business Management
- International and Foreign Markets
- International and Foreign Marketing
- International Marketing Management
  - Cross-cultural Issues in International Management

- UNIVERSITÀ DEGLI STUDI DI MILANO, Milano, Italy   1979
  Fulbright Scholar. Studied economics and international affairs

- CORNELL UNIVERSITY, Ithaca, NY   1976–1978
  B.A., *cum laude*, Native American Studies
      minor: economics and international relations

  Activities:

    - *President*, Class of 1978
    - *Co-captain*, Varsity Lacrosse, 1977, 1978
    - *President*, Alpha Omega Psi Fraternity, 1977

Affiliations

- American Marketing Association
- Sales and Marketing Executives International
- Marketing Research Association
- National Congress of American Indians
- League of the Six-Iroquois Nations in New York State and Canada
- The Pre-Columbian Powhattan Confederacy–East Coast
- The All-Pueblo Council in the Southwest

Interests

- Native American languages, history, art, and music
- Italian Renaissance opera and dance

Engineering   CHAUNCEY MERRILL THIGPEN

Professional Engineer _____
    4 Landsdowne Court • Houston, TX 77008 • 713/555-2222 (messages) •
    Fax: 713/555-0000 • E-mail: cthigpen.air.com

OBJECTIVE

A chemical engineering position in project development, including equipment specification, procurement, cost control, project scheduling, and installation.

EXPERIENCE

Project Engineer, Air Liquide, Houston, TX   1993–present
    Supervise industrial gas technology team of ten chemical engineers in
    development and production of oxygen, nitrogen, and carbon dioxide

Process Engineer, PPG Industries, Pittsburgh, PA   1992–1993
    Researched impact of production of chlorine and caustic soda on
    sub-tropical environments

Hoescht Celanese, Somerville, NJ   1990–1992
    Researcher. Developed specialty chemicals for Crayola© Crayons

    Associate Chemist. Monitored tests of pigments used in Tupperware
        and Rubbermaid products

    Assistant Chemist. Monitored tests of printing inks for _National
        Geographic Magazine_

ENGINEERING REGISTRATION

Fundamentals of Engineering Examination (1986)

Principles of Practice of Engineering Education (Texas/1995)

EDUCATION

Ph.D., 1991, University of Minnesota, Minneapolis, MN
    Major: chemical engineering
    Dissertation: ''Case studies in the use of photogrammetry in retrofit projects''
    Coursework: • Computational Methods in Chemical Engineering and
                    Material Science
                • Principles of Chemical Engineering
                • Unit Operations and Separation Processes
                • Scientific Models for Engineering Processes

Coursework: • Advanced Mathematics for Chemical Engineers
(cont'd) • Physical and Chemical Thermodynamics
• Chemical Reaction Kinetics—Kinetics of Homogeneous Reactions
• Chemical Reaction Analysis
• Chemical Engineering Laboratory
• Process Evaluation and Design
• Process Control
• Research in Chemical Engineering

B.Sc. 1986, University of Illinois at Urbana–Champaign, Urbana, IL
Major: chemical engineering

PRESENTATION

''Refinery Optimization Using Total Site (Pinch) Technology and Simulation Specification Data Sheets,'' CHEMPUTERS, Conference and Exhibition of Computer Technology for Chemical Engineers, Houston, TX, 14, 15 February 1996.

PUBLICATIONS

C. M. Thigpen, ''Process simulation. The art and science of modeling. A powerful engineering tool,'' *Chemical Engineering*, 101, 10, 82 (1994).

Thigpen, Chauncey M. *Catalytic Liquid Phase Hydrogenation*. New York: McGraw-Hill, 1995.

SKILLS/ABILITIES

Technical: LANs; WANs; client-server, object-oriented; C++; Visual BASIC; COBOL; NonStop SQL; TCP/IP; OLTP; UNIX; POSIX; MS DOS Windows

Highly developed teamwork abilities; superior communication, leadership, and flexibility skills.

AFFILIATIONS

American Chemical Society
American Institute of Chemical Engineers

REFERENCES

Available upon request

General Medicine

GENEVIEVE MARGARET ACKERMAN, M.D.

Director, University Health Services
University of Montana
Missoula, MT 59812
    (406) 555-7906
Fax: (406) 555-8291

SPECIALTY

General and Family Practice
    Subspecialty: community health

EDUCATION

- BROWN UNIVERSITY   Providence, RI
  M.D. 1986 Program in Medicine
    Clerkships:
    —Acute care.   Roger Williams General Hospital
        Providence, RI
    —Pediatrics.   The Emma Pendleton Bradly Hospital
        Providence, RI
- DARTMOUTH MEDICAL SCHOOL   Hanover, NH
  1984 The Brown-Dartmouth Program in Medical Education

Coursework

Year I		Year II	
Anatomy	Microbiology	Psychiatry	Epidemiology
Biochemistry	Neuroscience	Pharmacology	Clinical History
Cell Biology	Pathology	Physical Diagnosis	
Human Genetics	Physiology	The Scientific Basis of Medicine	

- BRYN MAWR COLLEGE   Bryn Mawr, PA
  1983 Postbaccalaureate Premedical Program

- UNIVERSITY OF MISSOURI–COLUMBIA   Columbia, MO
  1979 A.B. *magna cum laude*
    Major: anthropology
    Minor: journalism
        Honor: **Phi Beta Kappa**

CERTIFICATION and LICENSURE

- 1991 Medical License, State of Missouri
- 1990 Medical License, State of Montana
- 1985 American Board of Family Practice
- 1984 Diplomate, National Board of Medical Examiners

GENEVIEVE MARGARET ACKERMAN, M.D.

INTERNSHIP and RESIDENCY

- UNIVERSITY OF NEVADA — Reno, NV
  1990 School of Medicine
  Internship in community health

- UNIVERSITY OF NEBRASKA — Omaha, NE
  1987 College of Medicine
  Residency in general and family practice

- GEORGE WASHINGTON UNIVERSITY — Washington, DC
  1988–1989 School of Medicine and Health Services
  Residency in internal medicine

EXPERIENCE

- UNIVERSITY OF MONTANA — Missoula, MT
  1994–present *Director*, University Health Services

- UNIVERSITY OF NORTH DAKOTA — Grand Rapids, ND
  School of Medicine
  1994–present *Visiting Assistant Professor*

- NBC NEWS — New York, NY
  1993–1994 *Research Assistant to Health Sciences Correspondent*

- NEW ENGLAND JOURNAL OF MEDICINE — Waltham, MA
  1992–1994 *Associate Editor*

AFFILIATIONS

- American Academy of Family Physicians
- American Medical Association
- National Association of Medical Writers

INTERESTS

- Scientific writing (medical); Go; white water rafting; Mayan art

Law

PIERCE S. STATLER III
Suite 1200, Carnegie Towers
1777 Fifth Avenue
Pittsburgh, PA 15275

Residence:
412-555-1921
Fax: 412-555-1801

Office:
412-555-0923
Fax: 412-555-5883

24-Hour Answering Service
412-555-1806

Member of the Bar: State of West Virginia, admitted 1990
State of Pennsylvania, admitted 1991

EDUCATION

WEST VIRGINIA UNIVERSITY, College of Law   Morgantown, WV
Juris Doctorate, June 1990

Honors and Awards: Order of the Coif
Arthur Ritz Kindon, Jr. Memorial Prize
for highest first year GPA
West Virginia Bar Merit Scholarship

Activities:
Editor, West Virginia University Law Review, 1988–1989
Editorial Assistant, National Coal Issue, Eastern Mineral
Law Foundation, Inc., 1987
Member. Moot Court Board, 1986
Intellectual Property Association
Phi Alpha Delta

UNIVERSITY OF OXFORD, Balliol College   Oxford, England
Rhodes Scholar
M. Phil., 1986
Course: economics
Activities: crew, football, debate

WEST VIRGINIA UNIVERSITY   Morgantown, WV
B.A., *summa cum laude*, 1986. Major in economics (GPA 4.02); minor in English and
international studies. Cumulative GPA 4.0.

Academic Awards:
Phi Beta Kappa
Omicron Delta Epsilon, national honorary society in economics

PIERCE S. STATLER III
–2–

LEGAL EXPERIENCE

SUPREME COURT OF THE UNITED STATES   Washington, DC

Law Clerk. Honorable Sandra Day O'Connor. Performed duties such as research, drafting, editing, proofreading, and verification of citations; drafted working opinions pursuant to her direction. 1989–1990.

LTV STEEL COMPANY   Pittsburgh, PA

Attorney. Legal Department. Manage staff of ten; expedite international legal matters of multinational corporation such as anti-dumping and countervailing duty laws; import exclusion proceedings and export licensing; bilateral trade agreements; and treaties and foreign laws. 1994–present.

GOODWIN & GOODWIN   Charlestown, WV

Associate. Researched and drafted memoranda concerning corporate matters vis-a-vis banking and commercial law; managed team of four associates who prepared briefs for public utilities seeking redress in labor issues. 1991–1993.

PUBLIC DEFENDER CORPORATION   Moundsville, WV

Consultant. Provided representation in consumer law. 1990.

PUBLICATIONS

International Trade and Protectionist Economies, *20 Yale L.J. 503* (1991).

Most Favored Nation Legislation and Free Market Economies, *18 Stan. J. Int. L. 339* (1992).

The Human Rights Conundrum, Political Expedience, and International Trade, *10 W. Virginia L. Rev. 6* (1994).

SKILLS SUMMARY

Expert oral and written communication skills; practical experience in administration, supervision, negotiation, teaching, training, and tutoring.

PIERCE S. STATLER III
–3–

AFFILIATIONS

AMERICAN BAR ASSOCIATION   Chicago, IL

    Young Lawyers Division.
       Chairperson. International Law Committee, 1994.

PENNSYLVANIA BAR ASSOCIATION   Pittsburgh, PA

WEST VIRGINIA BAR ASSOCIATION   Charlestown, WV

INTERESTS

Crew; physical fitness; music (Gregorian Chants); Impressionist painting.

≡ 9 ≡
Conclusion

I encourage you to use the information presented thus far in preparing your curriculum vitae and accompanying correspondence, and urge you to continue, throughout your life, the creative reflection that produced it. My hortatory tone notwithstanding, I trust you will use this experience as a springboard for continued reflection on who you are and what you want to do in the future.

Discerning readers of *How to Prepare Your Curriculum Vitae* will recall that the CV, at least as it has often been constructed and disseminated in academic circles, has always been viewed as an extension of notions of academic freedom. From this perspective it has been shielded from any trend toward standardization or orthodoxy, which has become the fate of the traditional résumé. Members of the academy have always insisted on describing their academic and work backgrounds without regard for any commonly agreed upon standards, except those promulgated by professional associations and learned and scientific societies. This practice has often resulted in CVs of unusual length and confusing organization.

There is, not surprisingly, some movement toward changing this situation. *How to Prepare Your Curriculum Vitae* is a significant part of this change. It emphasizes adherence to writing styles and documentation guidelines of professional associations and learned and scientific organizations, while at the same time encouraging the use of guidelines that affect the overall presentations of all information on the CV. These changes have largely been occasioned by the increasing use of CVs outside of the academy. Moreover, the pervasive use of electronic recording, storage, and transmission of information has also contributed to changes in the content and format of CVs.

I trust that the preparation of your CV and accompanying correspondence has been a rewarding experience for you. Best wishes for a full and rewarding life.

Appendix A

U.S. and Canadian Postal Abbreviations

United States

AL	Alabama	MT	Montana
AK	Alaska	NE	Nebraska
AZ	Arizona	NV	Nevada
AR	Arkansas	NH	New Hampshire
CA	California	NJ	New Jersey
CO	Colorado	NM	New Mexico
CT	Connecticut	NY	New York
DE	Delaware	NC	North Carolina
DC	District of Columbia	ND	North Dakota
FL	Florida	OH	Ohio
GA	Georgia	OK	Oklahoma
GU	Guam	OR	Oregon
HI	Hawaii	PA	Pennsylvania
ID	Idaho	PR	Puerto Rico
IL	Illinois	RI	Rhode Island
IN	Indiana	SC	South Carolina
IA	Iowa	SD	South Dakota
KS	Kansas	TN	Tennessee
KY	Kentucky	TX	Texas
LA	Louisiana	UT	Utah
ME	Maine	VT	Vermont
MD	Maryland	VI	Virgin Islands
MA	Massachusetts	VA	Virginia
MI	Michigan	WA	Washington
MN	Minnesota	WV	West Virginia
MS	Mississippi	WI	Wisconsin
MO	Missouri	WY	Wyoming

Canada

AB	Alberta	NS	Nova Scotia
BC	British Columbia	ON	Ontario
LB	Labrador	PEI	Prince Edward Island
MB	Manitoba	PQ	Québec
NB	New Brunswick	SK	Saskatchewan
NF	Newfoundland	YT	Yukon
NT	Northwest Territories		

Appendix B

Action Verbs for Use in Curricula Vitae

accelerated	attached	communicated	decided	encouraged
accommodated	attained	compared	defined	endorsed
accomplished	attended	completed	delegated	enlarged
accounted for	augmented	composed	delivered	enlisted
achieved	authored	conceived	demonstrated	ensured
acquainted	authorized	concluded	designated	entered
acquired	_____	condensed	designed	established
activated	_____	conditioned	determined	estimated
adapted	_____	conducted	developed	evaluated
added		conferred	devised	examined
adjusted	balanced	consolidated	diminished	excelled
administered	bolstered	constructed	directed	exchanged
advertised	boosted	consulted	disclosed	executed
advised	briefed	contracted	discontinued	exercised
advocated	budgeted	controlled	discovered	exhibited
aided	built	converted	dispatched	expanded
alphabetized	_____	convinced	displayed	expedited
altered	_____	coordinated	distributed	explained
analyzed	_____	copied	drafted	explored
anticipated		corrected	dramatized	extended
applied	calculated	counseled	_____	_____
appointed	catalogued	counted	_____	_____
appraised	caused	crafted	_____	_____
approved	chaired	created		
arbitrated	changed	critiqued	earned	familiarized
argued	checked	curtailed	economized	filed
arranged	classified	_____	edited	financed
assembled	cleared up	_____	educated	forecast
assessed	collected	_____	elected	foresaw
assisted	combined		eliminated	formulated
assumed	commanded	debated	employed	fostered

159

found	invested	observed	qualified	simplified
_____	investigated	obtained	_____	smoothed
_____	_____	opened	_____	solved
_____	_____	operated	_____	sought
_____	_____	ordered		spearheaded
gathered		organized	rated	specified
governed	joined	originated	received	spoke
graded	judged	overcame	recognized	sponsored
greeted	_____	oversaw	recommended	stabilized
grossed	_____	_____	rectified	started
grouped	_____	_____	reduced	stopped
guaranteed	_____	_____	regulated	straightened
guided	labored		related	streamlined
_____	launched	paid	removed	strengthened
_____	lectured	painted	renovated	stripped
_____	led	participated	reorganized	studied
	located	perceived	repaired	submitted
handled	_____	performed	replaced	suggested
hastened	_____	persuaded	reported	supervised
heightened	_____	pioneered	rescued	supplemented
helped		planned	researched	surpassed
highlighted	maintained	policed	restored	_____
_____	managed	prepared	resulted in	_____
_____	mapped out	prescribed	returned	_____
_____	maximized	presented	revealed	
	measured	prevailed	reviewed	taught
identified	merged	processed	revised	terminated
illustrated	minimized	procured	_____	trained
implemented	modernized	produced	_____	transferred
improved	modified	profited	_____	transformed
included	monitored	programmed		_____
incorporated	motivated	prohibited	saved	_____
increased	_____	projected	scouted	_____
informed	_____	promoted	screened	
initiated	_____	proofed	scrutinized	unified
innovated		proved	selected	updated
inspected	negotiated	publicized	sent	utilized
instructed	netted	published	served	_____
interpreted	notified	purchased	set	_____
interviewed	_____	_____	shipped	_____
introduced	_____	_____	showed	
inventoried	_____	_____	sifted	vetoed

Appendix C

Selected U.S. and Canadian Professional, Learned, and Scientific Societies

UNITED STATES[1]

Anthropology

American Anthropological
 Association
4350 N. Fairfax Drive
Suite 640
Arlington, VA 22203
Tel: (703) 528-1902
Fax: (703) 528-3546

Archaeology

Archaeological Institute of America
675 Commonwealth Avenue
Boston, MA 02215-1401
Tel: (617) 353-9361
Fax: (617) 353-6550

Architecture

American Institute of Architects
1735 New York Avenue, NW
Washington, DC 02215-5292
Tel: (202) 626-7300
Fax: (202) 626-7420

Arts, The

American Council for the Arts
1 East 53rd Street
New York, NY 10022-4201
Tel: (212) 223-2787
Fax: (212) 223-4415

Biology

American Institute of Biological
 Sciences
730 11th Street, N.W.
Washington, DC 20001–4521
Tel: (202) 628-1500
Fax: (202) 628-1509

Chemistry

American Chemical Society
1155 Sixteenth Street, N.W.
Washington, DC 20036
Tel: (202) 872-4600
Fax: (202) 872-4615

---

1. *National Trade and Professional Associations of the United States*. Washington, DC: Columbia Books, Inc., 1994.

Computer Science

Computing Research Association
1875 Connecticut Avenue, N.W.
Suite 718
Washington, DC 20009-5728
Tel: (202) 234-2111
Fax: (202) 667-1066

International Association for
    Computer Systems Security
6 Swarthmore Lane
Dix Hills, NY 11746
Tel: (516) 499-1616
Fax: (516) 462-9178

Dentistry

American Dental Association
211 East Chicago Avenue
Chicago, IL 60611-2678
Tel: (312) 440-2500
Fax: (312) 440-7494

Economics

American Economic Association
2014 Broadway
Suite 305
Nashville, TN 37203-2418
Tel: (615) 322-2595
Fax: (615) 343-7590

Geography

American Geographical Society
4220 King Street
Alexandria, VA 22302
Tel: (703) 379-2480
Tel: (703) 379-7563

Geology

American Geological Institute
4220 King Street
Alexandria, VA 22302
Tel: (703) 379-2480
Fax: (703) 379-7563

American Geophysical Union
2000 Florida Avenue, N.W.
Washington, DC 20009
Tel: (202) 462-6900
Fax: (202) 328-0566

History

American Historical Association
400 A Street, S.E.
Washington, DC 20003
Tel: (202) 544-2422

Language

Modern Language Association of
    America
10 Astor Place
New York, NY 10003-6981
Tel: (212) 475-9500
Fax: (212) 477-9863

Law

American Bar Association
750 North Lake Shore Drive
Chicago, IL 60611-6281
Tel: (312) 988-5000
Fax: (312) 988-6281

Linguistics

Linguistic Society of America
1325 Eighteenth Street, N.W.
Suite 211
Washington, DC 20036-6501
Tel: (202) 835-1714

Mathematics

Mathematical Association of America
1529 Eighteenth Street, N.W.
Washington, DC 20036
Tel: (202) 387-5200

Medicine

American Medical Association
515 N. State Street
Chicago, IL 60610-4377
Tel: (312) 464-5000
Fax: (312) 464-4184

Music

American Society of Music Arrangers
 & Composers
P.O. Box 11
Hollywood, CA 90078
Tel: (213) 658-5997

International Association of
 Jazz Educators
P.O. Box 724
Manhattan, KS 66502
Tel: (913) 776-8744

Philosophy

American Philosophical Society
104 South Fifth Street
Philadelphia, PA 19106-3387
Tel: (215) 627-0706
Fax: (215) 440-3436

Physics

American Institute of Physics
1 Physics Ellipse
College Park, MD 20740-3843
Tel: (301) 209-3030
Fax: (301) 209-0840

Political Science

American Political Science
 Association
1527 New Hampshire Avenue,
 N.W.
Washington, DC 20036
Tel: (202) 483-2512
Fax: (202) 483-2657

Psychology

American Psychological Association
750 First Street N.E.
Washington, DC 20002-4242
Tel: (202) 955-7600
Fax: (202) 336-5708

Religion

American Academy of Religion
1703 Clifton Road, N.E.
Suite G-5
Atlanta, GA 30329-4019
Tel: (404) 727-7920
Fax: (404) 727-7959

Sociology

American Sociological Association
1722 N Street, N.W.
Washington, DC 20036
Tel: (202) 833-3410
Fax: (202) 785-0146

Theatre

American Society for Theatre
 Research
Department of Theatre, Fine Arts
 Center
University of Rhode Island
Kingston, RI 02881-0824
Tel: (401) 792-5921
Fax: (401) 792-5618

Dramatists Guild
234 West 44th Street
New York, NY 10036
Tel: (212) 398-9366
Fax: (212) 944-0420

CANADA[2]

Architecture

Society for the Study of Architecture
  in Canada
Box 2302, Ste. D
Ottawa, ON K1P 5W5
Tel: (416) 961-9956
Fax: (416) 585-2389

The Royal Architecture Institute
  of Canada
55 Murray Street, Ste. 330
Ottawa, ON K1N 5M3
Tel: (613) 232-7165
Fax: (613) 232-7559

Ordre des architectes du Québec
1825 boulevard René-Lévesque ouest
Montréal, PQ II3H 1R4
Tel: (514) 937-6168
Fax: (514) 933-0242

Arts, The

Royal Canadian Academy of Arts
163 Queen Street E., Box 2
Toronto, ON M5A 1S1
Tel: (416) 363-9612
Fax: (416) 363-9612

Conseil de la peinture du Québec
911, rue Jean-Talon Est. Bur. 120
Montréal (Québec) H2R 1V5
Tel: (514) 279-5600

Biology

Canadian Federation of
  Biological Societies (CFBS)
104-1750 Courtwood Cres.
Ottawa, ON K2C 2B5
Tel: (613) 225-8889
Fax: (613) 225-9621
E-mail: cfbs@hpb.hwc.ca

Chemistry

The Chemical Institute of Canada
130 Stater Street, Suite 550
Ottawa, ON K1P 6E2
Tel: (613) 232-6252
Fax: (613) 232-5862

Cinema & Film

Academy of Canadian Cinema
  & Television/Académie
  cdne du cinéma et de
  la television
158 Pearl Street
Toronto, ON M5H 1L3
Tel: (416) 591-2040
Fax: (416) 591-2157

Canadian Film Institute/
  Institut cdn du film
2 Daly Avenue
Ottawa, ON K1N 6E2
Tel: (613) 232-6727
Fax: (613) 232-6315

Computers & Information Processing

Association of Professional Computer
  Consultants
2175 Sheppard Avenue E. Ste. 110
Willowdale, ON M2J 1W8
Tel: (416) 491-3556
Fax: (416) 491-1670

---

2. *Corpus Almanac & Canadian Sourcebook*. 3rd annual ed. Don Mills, Ontario: Southam Inc.,
  1995.

Canadian Alliance Against Software
  Theft (CAAST)
Canada Trust Twr.
161 Bay Street, Ste. 2700
Toronto, ON M5J 2S1
Tel: 1 (800) 263-9700 (English)
    1 (800) 267-2875 (French)
Fax: (416) 863-9500

Canadian Information Processing
  Society
430 King Street, W. Ste. 103
Toronto, ON M5V 1L5
Tel: (416) 593-4040
Fax: (416) 593-5184

Dentistry

Canadian Dental Association
1815 Vista Drive
Ottawa, ON K1G 3Y6
Tel: (613) 523-1770
Fax: (613) 523-7736

Economics

Canadian Economics Association
Department of Economics
University of Toronto
150 St. George Street
Toronto, ON M5S 1A1
Tel: (416) 978-6295
Fax (416) 978-6713

Geography

Canadian Association of
  Geographers/L'Association
  canadienne des géographes
Burnside Hall
McGill University
805 rue Sherbrooke ouest
Montréal, PQ H3A 2K6
Tel: (514) 398-4946
Fax: (514) 398-7437

Royal Canadian Geographical
  Society
39 McArthur Avenue
Vanier, ON K1L 8L7
Tel: (613) 745-4629
Fax: (613) 744-0947

Geology

Geological Association of Canada
Department of Earth Sciences
Memorial University of
  Newfoundland
St. John's, NF A1B 3X5
Tel: (709) 737-7660
Fax: (709) 737-4569

History

Canadian Historical Association/
  Société historique du Canada
395 Wellington Street
Ottawa, ON K1A ON3
Tel: (613) 233-7885
Fax: (613) 567-3110

Law

Canadian Bar Association/
  L'Association
  du Barreau canadien
50 O'Connor Street, Ste. 902
Ottawa, ON K1P 6L2
Tel: (613) 237-2925
Fax: (613) 237-0185

Linguistics

Canadian Linguistic Association
  Inc./L'Association
  canadienne de linguistique inc.
Experimental Phonetics Lab
New College
University of Toronto
Toronto, ON M5S 1A1
Tel: (416) 599-0973

Mathematics

Canadian Mathematical Society
577 King Edward Avenue, Ste. 108
Ottawa, ON K1N 6N5

Medicine

The Royal College of Physicians and
  Surgeons of Canada
774 Echo Drive
Ottawa, ON K1S 5N8
Tel: (613) 730-6201
Fax: (613) 730-8252

Association of Canadian Medical
  Colleges
774 Echo Drive
Ottawa, ON K1S 5P2
Tel: (613) 730-1204
Fax: (613) 730-1196

Music

Association of Canadian Women
  Composers/L'Assoc. des femmes
  compositeurs cdnes
Canadian Music Center
20 St. Joseph Street
Toronto, ON M4Y 1J9
Tel: (416) 239-5195

Black Music Association of Canada
55 Chester Hill Road
Toronto, ON M4K 1X4
Tel: (416) 463-8880
Fax: (416) 463-8880

Canadian League of Composers
20 St. Joseph Street
Toronto, ON M4Y 1J9
Tel: (416) 964-1364

Physics

Canadian Association of Physicists/
  Association canadienne des
  physiciens
151 Slater Street, Ste. 903
Ottawa, ON K1P 5H3
Tel: (613) 237-3392
Fax: (613) 238-1677

Political Science

Canadian Political Science
  Association
1 Stewart Street, Ste. 205
Ottawa, ON K1N 6H7
Tel: (613) 564-4026

Sociology and Anthropology

Canadian Sociology and
  Anthropological Association
Concordia University
1445, boul. de Maisouneuve ouest
  bur. LB-615
Montréal (Québec) H3G 1M8

Appendix D

Selected Bibliography of Style Books and Manuals

American Psychological Association. *Publication Manual of the American Psychological Association*. 4th ed. Washington, DC: American Psychological Association, 1994.

American Society of Journalists & Authors Staff. *Tools of the Trade: Successful Writers Tell All about the Equipment & Services They Find the Best*. New York: HarperCollins, 1990.

Barzun, Jacques. *On Writing, Editing, and Publishing: Essays Explicative & Hortatory*. 2nd ed. Chicago: University of Chicago Press, 1986.

Becker, Howard S. *Writing for Social Scientists: How to Start and Finish Your Thesis, Book, or Article*. Chicago: University of Chicago Press, 1986.

The Bluebook: A Uniform System of Citation. Cambridge, MA: Harvard Law Review Association, 1991.

Brown, Bill Wesley. *Successful Technical Writing*. South Holland, IL: The Goodheart-Wilcox Co., Inc., 1993.

The CBE Manual for Authors and Publishers. Scientific Style and Format. 6th ed. Cambridge: Cambridge University, 1994.

Crewes, Frederick. *The Random House Handbook*. New York: McGraw-Hill, Inc., 1992.

DeBries, Mary A. *Prentice Hall Style Manual*. Englewood Cliffs, NJ: Prentice Hall, 1992.

Dodd, Janet S., and Marianne C. Brogan. *The ACS Style Guide: A Manual for Authors and Editors*. Washington, DC: American Chemical Society, 1986.

Dumond, Val. *The Elements of Nonsexist Usage*. New York: Prentice Hall Press, 1990.

Fowler, H. Ramsey and Jane E. Aaron. *The Little Brown Handbook*. HarperCollins, 1995.

Geological Survey (U.S.). Branch of Eastern Technical Reports. *A Guide for Preparing and Typing Geologic Division Book Manuscripts*. Reston, VA: U.S. Geological Survey, 1989.

Gibaldi, Joseph. *MLA Handbook for Writers of Research Papers*. 4th ed. New York: Modern Language Association of America, 1995.

Jordan, Lewis. *The New York Times Manual of Style and Usage*. New York: Quadrangle/New York Times Book Co., 1976.

Karls, John B. and Ronald Szymanski. *The Writer's Handbook*. Lincolnwood, IL: National Textbook Co., 1994.

Kirszner, Laurie G. and Stephen R. Mandell. *The Holt Handbook*. 3rd ed. New York: Harcourt Brace, 1992.

Lerner, Marcia. *Writing Smart*. The Princeton Review. New York: Villard Books, 1994.

Longyear, Marie. *The McGraw-Hill Style Manual*. New York: McGraw-Hill, 1989.

Luey, Beth. *Handbook for Academic Authors*. rev. ed. Cambridge: Cambridge University Press, 1990.

Lynch, Patrick J. *Yale C/AIM WWW Style Manual*. New Haven, CT: Yale Center for Advanced Instructional Media, 1995.

Marins, Richard. *A Writer's Companion*. 3rd ed. New York: McGraw-Hill, 1995.

New York Public Library. *Writer's Guide to Style and Usage*. New York: HarperCollins, 1994.

Nickerson, Marie-Louise. *The Scribner Workbook for Writers*. Boston: Allyn and Bacon, 1995.

Rubens, Philip, ed. *Science and Technical Writing. A Manual of Style*. New York: Henry Holt, 1992.

Shelton, James H. *Handbook for Technical Writing*. Lincolnwood, IL: NTC Business Books, 1995.

Steinmann, Martin, and Michael Keller. *NTC's Handbook for Writers*. Lincolnwood, IL: NTC Publishing Group, 1995.

Strunk, William, Jr., and E.B. White. *The Elements of Style*. 3rd ed. New York: Macmillan Publishing Co., 1979.

Turabian, Kate L. *A Manual for Writers of Term Papers, Theses, and Dissertations*. 4th ed. Chicago: University of Chicago Press, 1973.

United Press International. *The UPI Stylebook*. 3rd ed. Lincolnwood, IL: National Textbook Co., 1995.

United States, Government Printing Office. *Manual for Style*. Washington, DC: Government Printing Office, 1973.

The University of Chicago Press. *The Chicago Manual of Style: The Essential Guide for Writers, Editors, and Publishers*. 14th ed. Chicago: University of Chicago Press, 1993.

Williams, Joseph M. *Style: Toward Clarity and Grace*. Chicago: University of Chicago Press, 1990.

Zacharias, Johanna. *A Style Guide for CBD*. Washington, DC: Congress of the U.S., Congressional Budget Office, 1984.

Zinsser, William K. *On Writing Well*. 5th ed. New York: HarperCollins, 1992.

_____. *Writing to Learn*. New York: Harper and Row, 1989.

Appendix E

Selected Resources on Accompanying Correspondence

Adams, Robert L., ed. *The Adams Cover Letter*. Holbrook, MA: Adams Publishing, 1995.

Asher, Donald. *The Overnight Job Change Letter*. Berkeley: Ten Speed Press, 1994.

Beatty, Richard H. *175 High Impact Cover Letters*. New York: John Wiley & Sons, Inc., 1992.

———. *The Perfect Cover Letter*. New York: John Wiley & Sons, 1989.

Besson, Fannee. *Cover Letters*. New York: John Wiley & Sons, 1995.

Burgett, Gordon. *The Writer's Guide to Query Letters and Cover Letters*. Rocklin, CA: Prima Publishing, 1992.

Effective Letters for Business, Professional and Personal Use. Perrysburg, OH: Neal Publications, Inc., 1994.

Farr, J. Michael. *The Quick Resume and Cover Letter Book*. Indianapolis: JIST Works, 1994.

Fein, Richard. *Cover Letters! Cover Letters! Cover Letters!* Hawthorne, NJ: Career Press, 1994.

Frank, William S. *200 Letters for Job Hunters*. Berkeley: Ten Speed Press, 1993.

Hansen, Katherine and Randall Hansen. *Dynamic Cover Letters*. Berkeley: Ten Speed Press, 1995.

Kaplan, Bonnie Miller. *Sure-Hire Cover Letters*. New York: American Management Association, 1994.

Krannich, Ronald L. and Caryl Rae Krannich. *Dynamic Cover Letters*. 2nd ed. Manassas Park, VA: Impact Publications, 1991.

Krannich, Ronald L. and William J. Banis. *High Impact Resumes and Letters*. 6th ed. Manassas, VA: Impact Publications, 1995.

Marler, Patty and Jan Bailey Mattia. *Cover Letters Made Easy*. Lincolnwood, IL: VGM Career Horizons, 1996.

Martin, Eric R. and Karyn E. Langhorne. *How to Write Successful Cover Letters*. Lincolnwood, IL: VGM Horizons, 1995.

Provenzano, Steven. *Top Secret Resumes to Cover Letters*. Dearborn, MI: Financial Publishing, Inc., 1995.

Wynett, Stanley. *Cover Letters That Will Get You the Job You Want*. Cincinnati: Better Way Books, 1993.

Appendix F

Selected Fields of Graduate Study[1]

NATURAL SCIENCE

Agriculture
Agricultural Economics
Agricultural Production
Agricultural Sciences
Agronomy
Animal Science
Fishery Sciences
Food Sciences
Forestry and Related Sciences
Horticulture
Resource Management
Parks and Recreation Management
Plant Sciences
Renewable Natural Resources
Soil Sciences
Wildlife Management

Biological Sciences
Anatomy
Bacteriology
Biochemistry
Biology
Biometry
Biophysics
Botany
Cell and Molecular Biology
Ecology
Embryology
Entomology and Parasitology
Genetics
Marine Biology
Microbiology
Neurosciences
Nutrition
Pathology
Pharmacology
Physiology
Radiobiology
Toxicology
Zoology

Chemistry
Chemistry, General
Analytical Chemistry
Inorganic Chemistry
Organic Chemistry
Pharmaceutical Chemistry
Physical Chemistry

---

1. Graduate Record Examinations Board and the Council of Graduate Schools. *Directory of Graduate Programs*. 13th ed. Princeton: Educational Testing Service, 1991.

Computer and Information Science
Computer Programming
Computer Sciences
Data Processing
Information Sciences
Microcomputer Applications
Systems Analysis

Earth, Atmospheric, and Marine Sciences
Atmospheric Sciences
Environmental Sciences
Geochemistry
Geology
Geophysics and Seismology
Paleontology
Meteorology
Oceanography

Health and Medical Sciences
Allied Health
Audiology
Chiropractic
Dental Sciences
Environmental Health
Epidemiology
Health Science Administration
Immunology
Medical Sciences
Nursing
Optometry
Osteopathic Medicine
Pharmaceutical Sciences
Podiatry
Pre-Medicine
Public Health
Veterinary Medicine
Occupational Therapy
Physical Therapy
Speech/Language Pathology
Medicinal Chemistry
Veterinary Sciences

Mathematical Sciences
Actuarial Sciences
Applied Mathematics
Mathematics
Probability and Statistics

Physics and Astronomy
Astronomy

Astrophysics
Atomic/Molecular Physics
Nuclear Physics
Optics
Planetary Science
Solid State Physics
Physics

ENGINEERING

Engineering—Chemical
Chemical Engineering
Pulp and Paper Production
Wood Science

Engineering—Civil
Architectural Engineering
Civil Engineering
Environmental/Sanitary Engineering

Engineering—Electrical and Electronics
Computer Engineering
Communications Engineering
Electrical Engineering
Electronics Engineering

Engineering—Industrial
Industrial Engineering
Operations Research

Engineering—Materials
Ceramic Engineering
Materials Engineering
Materials Science
Metallurgical Engineering

Engineering—Mechanical
Engineering Mechanics
Mechanical Engineering

Engineering—Other
Aerospace Engineering
Agricultural Engineering
Biomedical Engineering
Engineering Physics
Engineering Science
Geological Engineering
Mining Engineering
Naval Architecture and Marine Engineering
Nuclear Engineering
Ocean Engineering

Petroleum Engineering
Systems Engineering
Textile Engineering

BUSINESS

Accounting
Accounting
Taxation

Banking and Finance
Commercial Banking
Finance
Investments and Securities

Business Administration and Management
Business Administration and Management
Human Resource Development
Institutional Management
Labor/Industrial Relations
Management Science
Organizational Behavior
Personnel Management

Business—Other
Business Economics
International Business Management
Management Information Systems
Marketing and Distribution
Marketing Management and Research

SOCIAL SCIENCES

Anthropology and Archaeology
Anthropology
Archaeology

Economics
Economics
Econometrics

Political Science
International Relations
Political Science and Government
Public Policy Studies

Psychology
Clinical Psychology
Cognitive Psychology
Community Psychology
Comparative Psychology
Counseling Psychology
Developmental Psychology
Experimental Psychology
Industrial and Organizational Psychology
Personality Psychology
Physiological Psychology
Psycholinguistics
Psychometrics
Psychopharmacology
Quantitative Psychology
Social Psychology
Psychology

Sociology
Demography
Sociology

Social Sciences—Other
Area Studies
Criminal Justice/Criminology
Geography
Public Affairs
Urban Studies
American Studies
Gerontology

EDUCATION

Education—Administration
Educational Administration
Educational Supervision

Education—Curriculum and Instruction
Curriculum and Instruction

Education—Early Childhood
Early Childhood Education

Education—Elementary
Elementary Education
Elementary Level Teaching Fields

Education—Evaluation and Research
Educational Statistics and Research
Educational Testing, Evaluation, and Measurement
Educational Psychology
Elementary and Secondary Research
Higher Education Research
School Psychology

Education—Higher
Educational Policy
Higher Education

Education—Secondary
Secondary Education
Secondary Level Teaching Fields

Education—Special
Education of Gifted Students
Education of Handicapped Students
Education of Students with Specific
    Learning Disabilities
Remedial Education
Special Education

**Education—Student Counseling and
    Personnel Services**
Personnel Services
Student Counseling

Education—Other
Adult and Continuing Education
Bilingual/Crosscultural Education
Educational Media
Junior High/Middle School Education
Pre-Elementary Education
Social Foundation
Teaching English as a Second Language
Agricultural Education
Physical Education
Vocational/Technical Education

ARTS

Arts—History, Theory, and Criticism
Art History and Criticism
Music History, Musicology, and Theory

Arts—Performance and Studio
Art
Dance
Drama/Theatre Arts
Music
Design
Fine Arts

HUMANITIES

English Language and Literature
English Language and Literature
American Language and Literature
Creative Writing

Foreign Languages and Literature
Asian Languages
Foreign Literature
French
German Languages
Italian
Russian
Semitic Languages
Spanish
Classical Languages

History
American History
European History
History of Science

Philosophy
All Philosophy Fields
Classics
Comparative Language and Literature
Linguistics
Religious Studies

OTHER FIELDS

**Architecture and Environmental
    Design**
Architecture
City and Regional Planning
Environmental Design
Interior Design
Landscape Architecture
Urban Design

Communications
Advertising
Communications Research
Journalism and Mass Communications
Public Relations
Radio, TV, and Film
Speech Communication

Home Economics
Consumer Economics
Family Relations
Family Counseling

Library and Archival Sciences
Library Science
Archival Science

Public Administration
Public Administration

Social Work
Social Work

Religion and Theology
Religion
Theology

The *Directory of Graduate Programs* includes information provided by nearly 800 accredited graduate institutions in the United States. Graduate programs leading to such traditionally professional degrees as J.D., D.D.S., D.V.M., and M.D. are not included. Each volume includes an index of programs that references entries in all four volumes, which are given below.

Volume A: Natural Sciences
Volume B: Engineering ■ Business
Volume C: Social Sciences ■ Education
Volume D: Arts ■ Humanities ■ Other Fields

Another comprehensive source of information on graduate programs is the six-volume *Peterson's Annual Guides to Graduate Study*, which offers information on more than 28,000 degree-granting graduate and professional programs at more than 1500 accredited colleges and universities in the United States and Canada.

- Book 1, *Graduate and Professional Programs; An Overview*. 29th ed. Princeton: Peterson's Guides, 1995.

- Book 2, *Graduate Programs in the Humanities and Social Sciences*. 29th ed. Princeton: Peterson's Guides, 1995.

- Book 3, *Graduate Programs in the Biological and Agricultural Sciences*. 29th ed. Princeton: Peterson's Guides, 1995.

- Book 4, *Graduate Programs in the Physical Sciences and Mathematics*. 29th ed. Princeton: Peterson's Guides, 1995.

- Book 5, *Graduate Programs in Engineering and Applied Sciences*. 29th ed. Princeton: Peterson's Guides, 1995.

- Book 6, *Graduate Programs in Business, Education, Health, and Law*. 29th ed. Princeton: Peterson's Guides, 1995.

Peterson's Graduate Education Database is on CD-ROM (The New Peterson's CD and CD-ROM from Silver Platter) and on-line through Dialog Information Retrieval Service, File 273.